Cambridge Elements

Elements in Leadership
edited by
Ronald E. Riggio
Claremont McKenna College
Susan E. Murphy
University of Edinburgh
Georgia Sorenson
University of Cambridge

LEADERSHIP BY EXAMPLE

Edward A. David
*University of Oxford
King's College London*

Shaftesbury Road, Cambridge CB2 8EA, United Kingdom

One Liberty Plaza, 20th Floor, New York, NY 10006, USA

477 Williamstown Road, Port Melbourne, VIC 3207, Australia

314–321, 3rd Floor, Plot 3, Splendor Forum, Jasola District Centre, New Delhi – 110025, India

103 Penang Road, #05–06/07, Visioncrest Commercial, Singapore 238467

Cambridge University Press is part of Cambridge University Press & Assessment, a department of the University of Cambridge.

We share the University's mission to contribute to society through the pursuit of education, learning and research at the highest international levels of excellence.

www.cambridge.org
Information on this title: www.cambridge.org/9781009498401

DOI: 10.1017/9781009498395

© Edward A. David 2025

This publication is in copyright. Subject to statutory exception and to the provisions of relevant collective licensing agreements, no reproduction of any part may take place without the written permission of Cambridge University Press & Assessment.

When citing this work, please include a reference to the DOI 10.1017/9781009498395

First published 2025

A catalogue record for this publication is available from the British Library

ISBN 978-1-009-49840-1 Hardback
ISBN 978-1-009-49836-4 Paperback
ISSN 2631-7796 (online)
ISSN 2631-7788 (print)

Cambridge University Press & Assessment has no responsibility for the persistence or accuracy of URLs for external or third-party internet websites referred to in this publication and does not guarantee that any content on such websites is, or will remain, accurate or appropriate.

For EU product safety concerns, contact us at Calle de José Abascal, 56, 1°, 28003 Madrid, Spain, or email eugpsr@cambridge.org

Leadership by Example

Elements in Leadership

DOI: 10.1017/9781009498395
First published online: June 2025

Edward A. David
University of Oxford
King's College London

Author for correspondence: Edward A. David, edward.david@kcl.ac.uk

Abstract: This Element offers a portrait of leadership exemplars in UK finance. It challenges the common trope that finance is morally bankrupt. More significantly, it provides an empirically informed account of what it means to lead ethically and by example. Drawing upon Linda Zagzebski's philosophy of moral exemplarism, as well as Braun and Clarke's reflexive approach to thematic analysis, this Element sifts through a rich interview dataset to identify three types of exemplary leader. The sage exemplifies a purpose-giving wisdom. The hero is admired for a courageous form of empathy. And the novice, an underappreciated type of exemplar, is singled out for curiosity. Foregrounding the place of positive emotions in role modeling, this Element sheds light on the virtues and psychology of leading by example. It also serves as an exemplar of what the humanities can contribute to the dynamic field of leadership studies.

Keywords: positive leadership, Linda Zagzebski, role model, thematic analysis, finance

© Edward A. David 2025

ISBNs: 9781009498401 (HB), 9781009498364 (PB), 9781009498395 (OC)
ISSNs: 2631-7796 (online), 2631-7788 (print)

Contents

1 Introduction   1

2 Theory and Reflexive Thematic Analysis   4

3 Novices Embrace and Question Admiration   16

4 Heroes Connect Empathy to Admiration   28

5 Sages Support Admiration through Organization   40

6 Conclusion   53

   References   58

1 Introduction

If there are ethical leaders in finance, the evidence – it seems – is in short supply. The crimes of senior bankers continue to make headlines (Hurley, 2023). The leadership failures of the global financial crisis continue to haunt regulators (George, 2008; Skapinker, 2023; Brenton, 2024). And celebrity financiers, supposed leaders in their field, continue to amass fortunes in criminal charges (Hurtado, 2023; Stempel, 2023). In the public eye, leaders in finance appear morally bankrupt.

Perhaps due to entrenched narratives of immoral behavior, research on ethical leadership in finance is scarce. Why search for a needle (ethical leaders) in a haystack (finance) if that haystack is perpetually on fire (enter any financial crisis here)? Of course, there are notable outliers to this trend. Business ethicists inspired by the philosopher Alasdair MacIntyre suggest that finance leaders promote moral goods, including virtue itself, through financial activity (Sison, Ferrero, and Guitián, 2017; Rocchi, Ferrero, and Beadle, 2021). And Princeton lecturer J. C. de Swaan (2020) uses case studies featuring well-known senior bankers to challenge negative perceptions of the sector. These interventions brave the rough seas of public opinion. But more research is needed – especially if we wish to understand what ethical leadership looks like in daily practice and in a sector that is strongly characterized by amorality and vice.

Eager to advance our knowledge of ethical leadership (especially in places where it's least expected), this Element engages in an empirical and philosophical analysis to offer a portrait of exemplary leadership in finance. It stems from a larger qualitative study that involved interviews with over 120 professionals from four UK sectors – business, law, technology, and finance – and that sought to identify (i) *which* character strengths are needed for ethical leadership in those sectors and (ii) *how* those strengths of character are developed in sector organizations.

Of the focal sectors under investigation, finance is arguably the most notorious. Hence, in this Element, I seek to get to the moral heart of the matter. I blend qualitative technique with moral philosophy to analyze the ways in which ethical leadership is perceived by thirty-three finance interviewees. In particular, my analysis focuses upon a specific phenomenon of leadership: the emotion of admiration. In leadership contexts, admiration – I propose – is directed toward ethical leaders, and it typically results in imitation of the persons admired. In line with the larger study's guiding questions, I analyze the data to discern: (i) *who* participants admire, paying careful attention to their strengths of character and the contexts in which these strengths operate, and (ii) *how* admiration responds to the people admired. Imitation is typical, but it is not the only response possible: Critical reflection, apathy, resentment, or even rejection of exemplars may happen. Investigation of the admirable adds useful focus to a study of character and leadership in finance. It also strengthens our ability to identify, describe, and assess the leaders that participants say they admire.

To avoid not seeing the wood for the trees, let me highlight this Element's contributions to the dynamic field of leadership studies. First, this Element offers a novel theoretical lens – Leadership by Example (LBE) – that can be used to analyze and critically engage with the phenomenon of leadership. Grounded in Linda Zagzebski's (2017) philosophy of moral exemplarism, LBE views leaders as moral exemplars who influence followers through the emotion of admiration. Leadership by Example fits within current paradigms of positive leadership – for example, charismatic and transformational leadership – that identify role modeling as an important leadership behavior. That said, LBE deepens these paradigms by examining admiration in detail. In this Element, I follow Zagzebski's (2017, chapter 2) capacious understanding of admiration – interpreted as an emotion that (i) has an intelligible object, an exemplar; that (ii) portrays the object as admirable, as when the emotion of fear makes something fearsome; and that (iii) potentially motivates, moving one toward emulation of an admirable figure. While one might disagree with Zagzebski (viewing admiration instead as a mental state or a cognitive judgment), I think that Zagzebski's understanding suffices for present purposes – namely, to interrogate admiration's range of moral and psychological responses to admirable leaders.

A second contribution of this Element involves deploying LBE to identify specific types of leadership exemplar and, by extension, to suggest what leading by example should look like in a financial context – and perhaps in general. Through a systematic study of interview data, facilitated by Braun and Clarke's (2021) reflexive approach to thematic analysis, this Element identifies three exemplar-types in UK finance. These are the novice, hero, and sage. Each is distinguished according to its central strength of character (curiosity, empathy, and wisdom) as well as specific domains of leadership in which each type excels (the self, teams, and organizations, respectively). Leadership by Example not only facilitates the identification and description of these exemplar-types, but it also invites reflection on whether these types – as objects of admiration – should be held in moral regard. According to Zagzebski (2017), we should trust admiration if it survives "conscientious self-reflection" and our "reflection over time" (p. 45). Leadership by Example adopts this ethical maxim since exemplars can only provide heuristics for morality (it is difficult, if not inadvisable, to copy them in every way) and since no exemplar is morally perfect (at least, this side of heaven). So, while much of this Element might read as a mere description, its detailed narratives begin a process of ethical reflection. It will be up to readers to decide whether the normative points raised are, or ought to be, "transferable" to their own practical settings and research agendas (Braun and Clarke, 2021, pp. 142–148).

Finally, this Element demonstrates how Braun and Clarke's method of thematic analysis can be used as a tool for humanistic study, both in general and for the philosophical analysis of leadership in particular. Embracing the interpretive expertise of researchers themselves, reflexive thematic analysis provides opportunities for scholars of the humanities – who typically excel in textual hermeneutics – to engage with empirical data in disciplinarily appropriate ways (Ciulla, 2019). Leadership studies would benefit from more interventions from the humanities; fortunately, thematic analysis gives philosophers, and anyone who relies on hermeneutics as a method, an accessible way into the field. This Element serves as an example of what is methodologically possible when qualitative research and philosophical analysis work together. Moreover, it serves as one of the only extended and worked examples of Braun and Clarke's method – which, despite its popularity, is one of the most misunderstood forms of thematic analysis, due in part to a lack of extended examples (Byrne, 2022).

With these contributions in mind, I have organized this Element as follows. Section 2 begins as any qualitative endeavor would: Following my research questions, Section 2 describes the empirical design. I cover the standard components, including participant sample, procedure of data collection, and analytical method. I also describe my theoretical commitments in detail: This effort abides by best practice in reflexive thematic analysis, and it foregrounds my philosophical interpretation of this qualitative method.

With my theoretical commitments made plain, the presentation of my analysis starts in Section 3 and ends in Section 5. Each of these sections offers a detailed narrative of my analytical themes – namely, the novice (Section 3), hero (Section 4), and sage (Section 5). Each theme, or leadership-type, speaks to my refined research questions, revealing *who* participants admire and *how* admiration responds vis-à-vis these exemplar-types. My narratives combine descriptive analysis (of what participants say is the case) with normative engagement (particularly from a virtue perspective). This blending of description and prescription is a function of Zagzebski's (2017) theory of moral exemplarism; though, as I explain in Section 2, it also follows from the normative aims of reflexive thematic analysis.

Section 6 concludes by summarizing this Element's themes, including its exemplarist and methodological insights. It also suggests how my theoretical lens, LBE, may be deployed and developed to further advance our understanding of what it means to lead ethically – and by example.

2 Theory and Reflexive Thematic Analysis

Let me start with an obvious, if underappreciated, claim: Every study that utilizes qualitative methods adopts a theoretical lens, or makes theoretical assumptions, to analyze its data (Malterud, 2016). Braun and Clarke (2021) identify two kinds of theory that inform qualitative analysis. The first is *big theory*. Big theory pertains to researchers' assumptions about "the nature of reality" (ontology) and "what constitutes meaningful knowledge," including "language and how it operates" (epistemology and interpretation) (p. 157). Situated at the broadest level, big theory encompasses all types of theory. In effect, it operates at the meta-theoretical domain. By contrast, *small theory* involves concepts and theoretical frameworks that are closer to the specific object of study. Given their own interests in gender and sexuality, Braun and Clarke (2021) associate small theory with political ideologies – such as queer theory and feminism – that underscore the influence of power in the production of knowledge (see also Clarke and Braun, 2019). Small theory, of course, can encompass a wider range of theoretical positions, from the theological (e.g., Christian ethics) to the literary (e.g., formalism). The exact choice of small theory will depend upon the subject matter at hand and, most significantly, upon researcher subjectivity. As Nowell et al. (2017) rightly note, "the researcher becomes the instrument for [qualitative] analysis" (p. 2).

In this section, I describe my theoretical assumptions, starting with the small theory and ending with the big (Sections 2.1 and 2.3), and I discuss empirical design (Sections 2.2 and 2.4). I begin with the small theory because its influence on my analysis will be obvious: Although developed relatively late in the analytic process, my small theory is used in a quasi-deductive manner; the entire analysis depends upon it. I then move to the big theory because, by understanding some of my meta-theoretical assumptions, readers can appreciate what sort of knowledge my analysis puts forward (empirical and philosophical) and hence may properly evaluate its analytic power as an interdisciplinary endeavor.

2.1 Leadership by Example

At the core of my "small" theoretical positioning is the emotion of admiration, which, as I explain in this section, is a characteristic emotion involved in learning from exemplars (Zagzebski, 2006, 2013, 2017). This emotion sits at the heart of my theoretical lens, LBE. Below, I outline three features of LBE; and, to elaborate upon its distinctiveness, I situate LBE conceptually within relevant literatures.

Broadly speaking, LBE does three things:

1. Leadership by Example identifies and describes *leadership exemplars*. A leadership exemplar is someone who, in an organizational context, elicits admiration with regard to a moral trait or behavior. Leadership by Example asks whether the emotion of admiration is present (Zagzebski, 2013) and, if so, to whom it is directed and why. Importantly, LBE does not treat leadership exemplars as moral saints, as if they can do no wrong. Rather, LBE views such exemplars as heuristics for moral learning (Bandura, 1977), despite their inevitable mistakes. Moreover, LBE does not restrict the phenomenon of leadership to formal roles: *Any* organizational actor could be a leadership exemplar. Leadership by Example also leaves open the possibility that technical achievements and talents can have moral relevance (cf., Algoe and Haidt, 2009). For instance, the intellectual abilities of a quant may inspire others to improve in a moral regard – for example, by inspiring followers to develop the virtue of perseverance to become closer to the quant in technical ability. No matter the kind of technical expertise involved, LBE considers leadership exemplars to be morally exemplary in some respect.
2. Leadership by Example identifies and describes *moral responses* to leadership exemplars. Not only does LBE attend to the objects of admiration (leadership exemplars), but it also draws attention to the subjects who feel the emotion of admiration (followers). Leadership by Example specifically observes the range of responses that subjects have toward leadership exemplars. Responses may include imitation, apathy, resentment, and even rejection of an exemplar outright or with regard to a perceived failing (Zagzebski, 2017). Not all these responses will follow from admiration, but if leaders are perceived to be admirable in some respect and at some time, then admiration is presumed to be involved to some extent. Whatever the case, LBE is open to a range of possible responses. It expects that context and the infinite variety of exemplars will challenge a simplistic or unitary account of moral responsiveness.
3. Leadership by Example prescribes what leadership exemplars, and moral responses to exemplars, *should be like* – albeit in a tentative manner, with its propositions subject to "conscientious self-reflection" and critical "reflection over time" (Zagzebski, 2017, p. 45). Whereas the first and second tasks of LBE seek evidence of admiration and of related responses, the third task of LBE is to engage with the evidence and to arrive at normative conclusions about leading by example. At this stage, LBE is conceived as a type or an application of moral theory. Leadership by Example draws upon Zagzebski's moral exemplarism specifically. But it may draw upon any number of moral theories as well – for example, Aristotelian virtue ethics or Kantian deontology.

With its central features outlined, one might ask whether LBE is a novel leadership construct – specifically when understood in a technical, social scientific sense. In short, it is not.

According to Hoch et al. (2018), a useful leadership construct is sufficiently distinct from existing scientific paradigms. It will enjoy (i) "conceptual non-redundancy," having distinctive theoretical grounds, and (ii) "empirical non-redundancy," illuminating distinct patterns of causality, correlation, and so on when empirically tested (p. 520). As I explain below, there is sound theoretical justification to distinguish LBE from existing leadership constructs in the social scientific literature. But since I have articulated LBE through a single qualitative study, it would be irresponsible to say that LBE already enjoys empirical nonredundancy. Scholarly application and inevitable refinements are now required.

That said, due to its distinct theoretical commitments, LBE has the potential to escape the dreaded realm of construct redundancy (Le et al., 2010). At minimum, it can be understood as a distinct theoretical lens, one that is useful for moral analysis. To substantiate this claim, I highlight two sets of literature, or sources, that contribute to LBE's distinctive character.

The first source covers existing constructs of positive leadership. Positive leadership is an umbrella term that accounts for leadership constructs that are associated with moral behavior. These typically include authentic leadership (Luthans and Avolio, 2003), charismatic leadership (House, 1977), ethical leadership (Brown, Treviño, and Harrison, 2005), servant leadership (Greenleaf and Spears, 2002), and transformational leadership (Bass and Riggio, 2006). Notably, leading by example is a *behavior* that is endorsed by many of these constructs: For instance, transformational leaders are said to influence followers as positive role models (Bass and Riggio, 2006), and ethical leaders are thought to model good conduct for their followers (Brown, Treviño, and Harrison, 2005).

Leadership by Example analyzes the behavior of "leading by example" through the lens of admiration. And instead of viewing this behavior as one part of a whole, LBE considers leading by example – specifically its central emotion, admiration – to be its primary focus or, more radically put, its *singular* point of departure (Zagzebski, 2017). This magnified perspective deepens our understanding of what "leading by example" means, as it adds emotional awareness to our analysis. Positive leadership constructs undoubtedly shine light on important aspects of leadership role modeling – from the way that transformational leaders improve followers' problem-solving skills (Mhatre and Riggio, 2014) to the role that leaders play in giving followers a sense of purpose (Kempster, Jackson, and Conroy, 2011). But, among their various limitations, many of these constructs view leadership role modeling from a narrow purview – one arguably constrained by rationalistic and leader-centric commitments.

In leadership contexts, rationalism construes role models as "cognitive construction[s]" (Gibson, 2004, p. 136) – or objects of "cognitive prompts" (Moberg, 2000, p. 678) – toward which followers must direct their *intellectual* efforts to learn. Leader-centrism supports this view in a significant way: Taking for granted a rationalist approach to learning, leader-centrism redirects our gaze from followers to the *leaders* who morally influence. In doing so, leader-centrism overlooks, and leaves under-analyzed, the ways in which followers' emotions influence moral learning. This omission is problematic. By failing to appreciate that followers need to *feel* admiration toward a possible exemplar, we do not help them *see* the person as a morally salient "cognitive construction" (Gibson, 2004, p. 136) – at least in a positive sense. Effective moral learning is thus undermined when an emotion like admiration is left unexamined. Leadership by Example seeks to avoid this situation by doubling down on this important affective dimension.

My focus on admiration brings us to a second source that contributes to LBE's theoretical distinctiveness – namely, the positive psychology of role modeling, including Zagzebski's philosophy of moral exemplarism. In contrast to the rationalist accounts previewed in this section, positive psychologists have eagerly explored the affective domain of role modeling, with scholars like Haidt (2003) instigating new strands of research into role modeling's moral emotions. This affective emphasis not only problematizes rationalistic conceptions of role modeling (challenging assumptions that moral development results only or primarily from deliberate rational efforts), but it also aligns with a trend of "emotional sensitization" (an awakening to moral development's affective plane) that features in contemporary research in moral education (Kristjánsson, 2017, p. 21). Although welcome, this trend does not have a strong presence in leadership studies or in the wider management literature.

One way to emotionally sensitize the field is to start from new conceptual grounds. Here, the work of Zagzebski is especially useful. Challenging conventional moralities, Zagzebski (2017) offers a comprehensive ethical theory built upon the admiration of exemplary figures. Moral exemplarism, she writes,

> [defines] all central terms in moral discourse including "virtue," "right act," "duty," and "good life," by direct reference to exemplars, or persons *like that*, where *that* is the object of admiration. (p. 3, emphasis in original)

Importantly, for Zagzebski, admiration is an emotion; and emotions, she claims, are not divorced from rationality. Indeed, emotions "are ways of affectively perceiving the world around us" (Zagzebski, 2004, p. 52). The perceptible objects of admiration appear "attractive, not repulsive or evaluatively neutral," and, once admired, they can elicit in us an "urge to imitate" the observed phenomenon (Zagzebski, 2017, p. 35) – for example, an admirable leader. Admiration thus construed constitutes the affective point of origin for Zagzebski's understanding of the role-modeling process in its central case: It begins with (i) admiration, which leads to (ii) a conception of oneself as lacking the admired qualities but desiring to possess them, which (iii) typically culminates in emulation.

Thus, Zagzebski affirms the connection that psychologists make between so-called elevating emotions and the imitation of moral exemplars (Haidt, 2003; Algoe and Haidt, 2009). From a descriptive point of view, examining this connection is worthwhile if only to deepen our understanding of role-modeling psychology. But Zagzebski's intentions go beyond mere description. As mentioned earlier, she foregrounds admiration to articulate a novel moral theory. On this front, Zagzebski does not think that moral theories must provide clear directions for moral decision-making. But she is convinced that a good moral theory is like a map – something that gives us an "understanding of the domain of morality as a whole" – which, in turn, can inform our "actual moral practice" (Zagzebski, 2017, p. 7). The following passage helps us appreciate why Zagzebski links moral theory with role modeling's central emotion. She writes:

> When a map is intended to be used for navigation, it cannot serve its purpose unless there is a motive to follow it. My theory [moral exemplarism] is intended to provide the motive for following the map. It might seem impossible that a theory can arise out of a motivating emotion – not the concept of an emotion, but an emotion itself, but that is what I am going to propose. The motivating element is at the root of the theory. Since admiration motivates emulation of admired persons, the theory is also useful for the purposes of moral education. I think it is a particular advantage of a theory if it can link up with narratives since narratives are one of the primary vehicles for the moral education of the young, and the basic way humans of any age develop and alter their moral sensibilities. Narratives capture the imagination and elicit emotions that motivate action. (Zagzebski, 2017, p. 8)

Leadership by Example accepts much of these theoretical and practically oriented commitments: It acknowledges the motivating force of admiration; it finds evidence of it in the stories finance professionals tell; and it aspires to guide moral practice through an orientation toward the admirable. I discuss these and other aspects of Zagzebski's theory in Section 2.3. For now, I turn to empirical design.

2.2 Empirical Design

In Section 1, I mentioned that the analysis presented within this Element stems from a larger qualitative study. That study investigated leadership and character in multiple UK industries and was initiated by the Virtues and Vocations research group based in the Faculty of Theology and Religion at the University of Oxford. I was a researcher of that group; and, with permission from the University which holds the project data, I here extend that initial investigation to explore the phenomenon of admiration – a central aspect of LBE – in finance. Let me say a few words about the research design of the larger study.

The Virtues and Vocations study sought to conduct, and analyze data from, interviews with over 120 professionals working across four industry sectors in the UK. The study posed two exploratory questions: (i) Which character strengths are needed for ethical leadership in those sectors, and (ii) how are those strengths of character developed in sector organizations? To explore character development in each sector, the study utilized a comparable case-selection approach (Goetz and LeCompte, 1984), seeking participants who could speak to a shared culture of industry activity. For the finance sector, participants were full-time employees of financial service firms that were either domiciled or had an active presence in the UK. Notably, most of the participants were sourced by firms themselves: Some banks asked individuals directly to participate; others sent firm-wide communications to secure volunteers. Whatever the means of recruitment, all firms abided by the study's purposive sampling strategy (Miles, Huberman, and Saldaña, 2020), which aimed to hear a diversity of voices within each organization. Moreover, all participants were reassured that their employers would not have access to the interview data and that their identities would remain anonymous. The extent to which firms and participants worried about incriminating information is unknown, but all were reminded of the study's research focus – character strengths and their development, not vices and scandals within their organizations. This positive approach likely encouraged many to participate.

In all, a total of thirty-three participants from a handful of financial service firms were interviewed. Some firms had fewer than fifty full-time employees; the remaining organizations had employee numbers in the tens of thousands. Total assets of all the organizations were valued in the hundreds of billions (£). The firms operated in a variety of financial subsectors, from alternative investments to retail banking. Individual participants were between the ages of twenty-four and sixty-two, with an average age of forty. Seventeen participants identified as female, and sixteen as male. Seventy-eight percent identified with a White ethnic background. Eight held junior positions, eight mid-level positions, and seventeen senior or executive positions.

As for the procedure of data collection, participants were interviewed individually and with informed consent via secure video call in the second half of 2021, during the coronavirus pandemic. Following a semistructured interview guide, researchers spoke with participants for an average of sixty minutes. The guide featured four sets of questions, regarding (i) participants' job roles; (ii) their organization's values; (iii) personal purpose, values, and character; and (iv) character development for future leaders. The guide also prompted researchers to ask participants directly about their leadership role models.

At the start of every interview, an introductory statement was read aloud, which helped to focus the conversation. The statement did three things. First, it made known the project's exploratory research areas (character strengths for leadership, and how firms develop these). Second, it demonstrated the practical value of participating in the research (the project would inform leadership development programs at the university level). Third, it signaled that the expert in the room was the participant: They were the focus of the conversation, their perspectives were what mattered. As interviews were completed, an authorized third party transcribed each recording verbatim. The transcripts were then cleaned and checked against the recordings to ensure accuracy. Pre- and post-interview field notes were made and compiled, and they too were added to the overall dataset. In total, the finance dataset consisted of over 400 A4-sized pages – a veritable treasure trove of leadership insights.

2.3 Philosophical Thematic Analysis

To analyze the data, I used a qualitative method, but I approached that method as a scholar of the humanities. My approach merits explanation. In brief, I view Big Q qualitative research – including research that uses reflexive thematic analysis – as exercises in philosophical interpretation. This position is justified by the emphasis on "meaning" in Big Q qualitative research (Braun and Clarke, 2021, p. 6) and by the fact that meaning is subject to interpretation – which is a domain of expertise in the humanities, especially philosophy (Ciulla, 2019). In this section, I elaborate upon this position with reference to my big theory commitments and to my use of reflexive thematic analysis.

To begin, let me offer a summary of Braun and Clarke's method. In their own words, reflexive thematic analysis is "an accessible and robust method ... for developing, analysing and interpreting patterns across a qualitative dataset, which involves systematic processes of data coding to develop themes" (Braun and Clarke, 2021, p. 4). It is reflexive in as much as the "subjective, situated, aware and questioning researcher, a *reflexive* researcher," is "fundamental" to the execution of thematic analysis (Braun and Clarke, 2021, p. 5, emphasis in original). Valued for their subjective expertise, the researcher approaches the data with some set of theoretical presuppositions – either determined from the start of a project or discovered in the analytic process "at some point" (Braun and Clarke, 2021, p. 158). Hence, reflexive thematic analysis takes a Big Q orientation toward qualitative research, embracing a variety of theoretical approaches to the data. In effect, it makes space for whatever philosophical positions the researcher aims to adopt.

There are at least two types of theoretical, or philosophical, choices that a researcher must make when engaging with reflexive thematic analysis. For the sake of simplicity, I describe these choices, including my own decisions, in terms of binaries. In reality, they exist along spectra (Byrne, 2022).

The first choice pertains to one's fundamental orientation toward qualitative data, specifically from an interpretive perspective. An (i) *experiential orientation* gives voice to participants' experiences: Here, a "hermeneutics of empathy" operates in order to make sense of the personal realities being expressed (Braun and Clarke, 2021, p. 160). By contrast, a (ii) *critical orientation* approaches data with the aim of interrogating them and examining "the effects and functions of [participants'] patterns of . . . meaning": a "hermeneutics of suspicion" is at work here (Braun and Clarke, 2021, p. 160).

In my analysis of the finance interviews, I adopted a hermeneutics of empathy. I wanted to make sense of what participants had to say about leadership role models; hence, I shaped my theoretical lens, LBE, so that it was useful for exemplar identification and description (Section 2.1). While it is tempting to view an empathic hermeneutics as descriptively naïve or merely summative of surface level statements, this characterization is far from the truth. To "make sense" of something is to invite deep reflection, an unpacking of terms, and an exploration of what participants say – and do not say – in their responses. These tasks are not confined to a hermeneutics of suspicion. In fact, empathy itself is understood as the extraordinary ability to enter into, and understand, another's emotional and intellectual world (Maibom, 2022). This is no easy task. A hermeneutics of empathy requires skill and sophistication, including a capacity to "stay close" to participant meanings, while developing those meanings in creative, even critical, ways – nevertheless, in ways that are "recognizable to [participants]" (Braun and Clarke, 2021, p. 160). Indeed, as a study in leadership, this Element is committed to presenting an analysis of exemplars that is both recognizable (reflecting participants' emotional and intellectual worlds) and surprising (revelatory about leadership in certain contextual respects).

A second theoretical choice for reflexive thematic analysis concerns ontology – a philosophical term that refers to the nature of some aspect of reality. Since Braun and Clarke's work investigates topics of ethical relevance (e.g., Braun et al., 2009; Pickens and Braun, 2018; Clarke and Braun, 2019), and given my focus on positive leadership, let me describe the theoretical options with respect to moral theory. A (i) *realist approach* to data assumes that moral truth exists out in the world, independent of human minds, and is discoverable by us. Moral realism is construed in various ways, typically with reference to physical nature, human reason, or a combination of both (Matava, 2011). A (ii) *relativist approach*, by contrast, "does not subscribe to the notion of a singular reality [or moral truth] that exists independent of human practices" (Braun and Clarke, 2021, p. 173). The ancient Greek sophists are associated, somewhat inaccurately, with this moral view (Bett, 1989).

My analysis is closer to the moral-realist end of the spectrum, but it certainly does not adopt a naïve realism, that is, an approach that "assumes that the [moral] world is [simply] as it appears to be" (Braun and Clarke, 2021, p. 169). Recall that LBE aims to prescribe what leadership exemplars, and moral responses to exemplars, should be like – albeit tentatively and subject to critical reflection. To do so, LBE must move beyond mere description and an uncritical, or even illogical, assertion that "what is" is "what ought-to-be." Avoiding this can take many forms. Zagzebski's theory of moral exemplarism – on which LBE is based – does this through Hilary Putnam's (1975) and Saul Kripke's (1980) philosophical accounts of direct reference: "all central terms in moral discourse including 'virtue,' 'right act,' ... are defined] by *direct reference* to exemplars[,] ... the object[s] of admiration" (Zagzebski, 2017, p. 3, emphasis added).

While it is not the aim of this Element to thoroughly explain or critique this part of Zagzebski's theory, we must appreciate upfront (i) that Zagzebski takes a semantic approach to morality (we *say* that exemplar *x* is an object of our admiration, and so we shape our collective moral *language* to reflect the exemplar) and (ii) that exemplars can be said to exist independently from human minds, and thus moral exemplarism displays a certain degree of moral realism (Zagzebski, 2017, chapter 8). Insofar as my small theory is inspired by Zagzebski, LBE can accept this semantically associated form of moral realism.

That said, as my analysis will make clear, I also rely on the concept of human flourishing – as understood through Aristotle (350 BC/2009) and Aquinas (1266/1964) – to explore the virtues of participants' exemplars more thoroughly. I do this for several reasons. First, the Aristotelian-Thomist tradition offers a ready store of conceptual riches concerning the virtues and their exemplars; its insights will help explain, verify, or challenge participant responses. Second, while LBE embraces Zagzebski's semantic approach to moral realism, there admittedly are philosophical difficulties in understanding how one can move from the "is" of a leader's example to the "ought" of leading by example. The

Aristotelian-Thomist tradition can help fill in some conceptual gaps. But I think that Zagzebski's theory has resources internal to it that help to clarify its semantic approach and help to appreciate why it can exist alongside Aristotelian-Thomist accounts of virtue: I address this point head-on in Section 6. At any rate, drawing upon Aristotle or Aquinas is in keeping with Zagzebski's (2017) claim that "there can be more than one equally good moral theory" (p. 9). Moral exemplarism is but one moral map, and "since maps always leave something out," we can – and should – pick up another map to enrich our moral vision (Zagzebski, 2017, p. 9).

So much for my big theory commitments. We now understand that my analysis stays close to participant experiences, while creatively interpreting and interrogating their claims. We also understand that my analysis is an exercise in moral realism, offering a vision for what leading by example could look like should we accept its propositions after "conscientious self-reflection" over time (Zagzebski, 2017, p. 45). This analysis may be categorized as social scientific. But a more accurate interpretation – if we are to be honest about the types of theoretical choices to be made – is that this Element's thematic analysis is philosophical. It is the happy artifact of humanistic study.

2.4 Theme Development

Readers may be eager for my thematic analysis to finally begin. I am, too. But, first, it is important to quickly outline the phases of Braun and Clarke's method of analysis, to note where in that process my philosophical commitments (including my small and big theories) were solidified, and – most importantly – to preview my study's three themes that I conceptualize as ideal *types* of leadership exemplar.

Braun and Clarke identify six phases in their reflexive approach to thematic analysis. From my philosophical perspective, I view these phases as falling within two broad stages: an empirical and descriptive stage (Phases 1–3), and a philosophical and prescriptive stage (Phases 4–6). I explain this additional layer below.

According to Braun and Clarke (2021), Phase 1 involves familiarizing oneself with the dataset. For me, this involved seemingly endless hours of reading and rereading interview transcripts. This was tedious at times, but a joy when the moral imagination was engaged. Phase 2 entails a systematic and fine-grained process of coding the data. Each of my codes aimed to capture a single concept or meaning that was relevant for the study's original research questions (regarding character strengths for leadership, and how firms develop these). Phase 3 involves an initial generation of themes, where the researcher identifies patterns of meaning that are evident across the entire dataset.

I approached this phase by clustering my codes – along with their accompanying data excerpts – into groups of shared meaning. Each group, or candidate theme, captured its own distinct meaning: For example, one of my early candidate themes was "founders' inspirational stories," which included data excerpts related to this analytic category. (This candidate was eventually incorporated into a more conceptually rich theme: see Section 5.)

Phases 1–3 of reflexive thematic analysis require tremendous patience, as they demand a close reading of the entire dataset. In my mind, these phases constitute what may be called an empirical and descriptive stage in the analytic process. Researchers must attend to the empirical evidence before them, and they must accurately describe what they see, regardless of whether they take an inductive or deductive approach to the data in the first instance. Reflexive researchers ideally recognize, and embrace, their theoretical assumptions during this first stage; but my own experience suggests that one can approach these phases with plenty of theoretical uncertainty. More pressing than theoretical surety is the practical need to code and cluster. As long as the initial research questions are accounted for, no deep philosophizing seems required.

Let us return to Braun and Clarke's description of the remaining phases. Phase 4 involves the assessment and continued development of themes. Good themes highlight an important pattern in the data (they tell a compelling story); they sit well with each other (they cohere in some way, even if they may surface contradictory insights); and, of course, they relate to the original research questions. Moreover, as Braun and Clarke (2021) stress, good themes engage with "existing knowledge, and/or practice[,] in [one's] research field, [including] the wider context of [one's] research" (p. 35). Phase 5 entails much of the same, except that researchers now need to finalize the names of their themes. And Phase 6 concludes the analytic process: Here, researchers weave the analysis together into a compelling narrative.

There are two points I wish to make about these phases. First, I interpret Phase 4 as initiating the philosophical, and even prescriptive, stage of reflexive thematic analysis. Researchers' engagement with "existing knowledge . . . and practice," and with "the wider context" of their research (Braun and Clarke, 2021, p. 35), does not necessarily mean that they will engage with philosophical literature or make good philosophical arguments. Nevertheless, this phase deliberately invites researchers to read widely and to think deeply about the connections between their dataset, relevant theories and evidence, and themselves as researchers. To encounter these connections is, ideally, to move beyond mere knowledge and to venture toward wisdom. *Philosophia*, the love of wisdom, is the path *and* destination. Moreover, because reflexive thematic analysis is inherently ethical – or political by Braun and Clarke's

(2021) lights – this stage does not preclude practical, moral considerations. Its analysis may very well be morally driven.

A second point follows. In the second stage of reflexive thematic analysis (Phases 4–6), researchers should not be surprised if their primary research questions evolve and if their theoretical commitments develop. In most cases, I would imagine that these aspects of the research *should* change – after all, Big Q qualitative analyses are iterative and far from static. With regard to theory, it was in Phase 4 where, confronted by an overwhelming amount of relevant literatures, I found Zagzebski's (2013, 2017) theory of moral exemplarism to be a guiding light: Its emphasis on the emotion of admiration helped me to make descriptive and moral sense of interviewees' remarks about their own strengths of character and those of exemplary leaders. Leadership by Example was developed from Phase 4 onwards; and, even at this later stage in the analytic process, I decided to use LBE in a quasi-deductive manner for its hermeneutic potential and even to test and develop moral exemplarism itself.

With regard to my research questions, the theoretical work done in Phases 4–6 empowered me to respond to the larger study's initial questions with refined questions of my own. No longer was I tempted to simply list (i) leadership character strengths and (ii) organizational means to develop them. (Braun and Clarke would certainly critique this simplistic use of reflexive thematic analysis.) Instead, I became philosophically attuned to the data so as to ask (i) who participants admired as leaders and in what domains, and (ii) how admiration responds – and ought to respond – in relation to those exemplars. This latter set of questions is built upon the former, and it invited me to respond to that former set in a focused and conceptually fruitful way. This privilege was afforded by the theoretical flexibility, including the philosophical orientation, of reflexive thematic analysis.

Now to my study's themes. In light of my refined research questions (concerning who participants admire and how admiration responds), I chose to conceptualize my themes as three types of leadership exemplar. These are the *sage*, whose purposeful leadership exemplifies practical wisdom at an organizational level; the *hero*, whose courage takes the perhaps unexpected form of empathy in team settings; and the *novice*, an underappreciated type of leader, whose moral curiosity inspires others to excel in leading their own selves. Following best practice in thematic analysis, each theme (or type) is accompanied by subthemes that, in my case, fill in the picture of what sages, heroes, and novices are like. As Braun and Clarke (2021) suggest, themes and subthemes are meant to convey from the data "a pattern of shared meaning, organised around a central concept" (p. 77). Moreover, themes and subthemes are meant to say something "analytically useful" for a study's research questions (Braun and Clarke, 2021, p. 113).

My themes, or types, certainly do both. They underscore the virtues that interviewees think are indispensable for leadership in finance (curiosity, empathy, and wisdom), including the domains in which those virtues operate (the self, teams, and the wider organization). Moreover, each type highlights how leading by example interacts with admiration: Novices underscore admiration's importance; heroes, how empathy and admiration relate; sages, the wise structures that support admirable effects. These are levels of analysis that my theoretical lens, LBE, helps to bring forward. Its exemplarist insights are summarized by subtheme in the discussion sections of Sections 3–5.

Let me conclude this section with a brief review. This section of the Element served two purposes. First, it provided an overview of the Element's qualitative research design, including its theoretical lens, LBE. Second, it interpreted its qualitative method – reflexive thematic analysis – as a philosophical tool. The section made the case that Big Q qualitative research and reflexive thematic analysis especially are best understood within a humanistic paradigm that relies on hermeneutics, or theory-driven interpretation, for its methodological strength. Leadership by Example is the hermeneutic lens of the present analysis; and, given its reliance upon Zagzebski's moral exemplarism, readers should expect descriptive and morally suggestive insights about positive leadership in finance.

Finally, a quick word about anonymity in my analytic presentation. In what follows, I take several measures to ensure that participant identities are hidden. First, no organizations or individuals are named, and I attribute a generic job role, organization, and/or subsector to each participant. With certain participants, I change their role, organization, and/or subsector altogether. Such changes are meant to protect identities, while retaining relevant context for the analysis. Second, I assign a number to each participant (P1, P2, and so on). Proximity in the sequential order does not necessarily indicate that participants are from the same organization (P3 and P4 may not belong to the same firm, for example). Third, I have removed all personally or institutionally identifying information from direct quotations. Without further ado, I turn to my first theme.

3 Novices Embrace and Question Admiration

I begin my analysis with a portrayal of an unexpected type of leader. Many are familiar with sages and heroes; their wisdom and courage precede them. But few appreciate *novices* – the morally curious – who excel in a deeply personal and moral form of self-leadership (Neck and Manz, 2013). This exemplar-type makes for an appropriate starting point for a study in LBE for at least two reasons.

First, the novelty of this type causes us to pay attention. In role-modeling studies, the term "novice" usually represents the *un*exemplary side of a "novice–exemplar relationship" (Vaccarezza and Niccoli, 2019, p. 340). But, as my analysis demonstrates, the novice-type represents a distinct and highly valued type of leader. Indeed, according to one participant, finance's ideal leaders – whether emerging or established in the C-suite – are novice-like in character: "I would want [leaders] to be curious. I would want them to ask questions and [to] feel okay [doing] that," the participant says (P13).

Second, the novice-type underscores the way in which leading by example depends upon admiration that, as scholars suggest, is at the affective origin of the role-modeling process (Zagzebski, 2017; see also Algoe and Haidt, 2009). That said, and as we will see, the novice-type does not fit neatly into an idealized or uncritical account of admiration. This type features individuals whose curiosity – while directed toward exemplars – does not approach admiration and modeled behaviors in an uncritical way. Novices ask questions, often difficult questions. Thus, this exemplar-type may well be the Socrates of the City, embodying what a reflexive and critical form of admiration should look like in actual practice.

In the analytic narrative that follows, I focus upon the novice's relevance for understanding admiration and admiration's place within the exercise of leading by example. I do this by exploring three subthemes, conceptualized as three sets of exemplarist propositions.

First, the curious prefer learning from exemplars. Between (i) abstract methods of moral development, for example, engagement with company values, and (ii) personal encounters with admirable leaders, novices typically choose the route of admiration (Section 3.1). Second, humility is a prerequisite virtue for curiosity. Novices succeed in sourcing morally relevant information because they are humble (Section 3.2). Third, curiosity needs moral guidance. A strong sense of integrity – aided by deep moral questioning – helps novices discern good examples from their vicious counterparts (Section 3.3). I summarize these propositions, and discuss the idea that novices are exemplary self-leaders, in the section conclusion (Section 3.4).

Before embarking on my analytic presentation, it is worth reiterating the following point: that my exemplarist claims are as descriptive as they are normatively suggestive. They are descriptive insofar as they convey what participants said in their interviews. But to the extent that they reflect participants' admiration of exemplary leaders (or even of their own selves), the claims may be appreciated for their normative valence. Following Zagzebski (2017), we can use these claims to define "central terms in [our] moral discourse" (including virtues or strengths of character) via "direct reference to exemplars" – or, more specifically, via direct reference to the exemplars of interviewees (p. 3). My analysis of novice-type – and of each leadership-type in this Element – simply begins a moral conversation. It is up to the reader to determine what to accept or reject, and to identify on what moral grounds to do so.

3.1 The Curious Prefer Learning from Exemplars

"[Future leaders] need curiosity," says a banking engineer (P8). And "curiosity's ... not just about career learning," says a retail analyst (P21). It involves "learning ... about yourself," an investment associate claims (P29). Echoed in diverse parts of the sector, this trio of sentiments neatly captures not only the importance of curiosity for novices but also two of curiosity's possible ends: professional development ("career learning") and personal growth ("learning ... about yourself").

Scholars of the intellectual virtues see curiosity as foundational for the attainment of various professional achievements (İnan, 2012; Watson, 2022) since it operates as a "mainspring of motivation" for technical endeavors (Miscevic, 2007, p. 246). But as the investment associate suggests, curiosity is foundational for personal and moral development, as well:

> Curiosity ... [has] been a big theme in my life for many, many years .... [In my] role, ... [I'm] always ... learning about different companies and businesses. But you're also learning a lot about yourself ... [I]n this industry, it's very easy to get caught up with stocks and numbers ... and being hyper-rational ... But ... there's some development [of] the human spirit [too]. (P29)

His firm in particular "sanction[s]," or endorses, moral curiosity by requiring attendance at reflective team away-days. During one of them, the associate recalls having "a little epiphany" about his own character strengths (P29). His experience suggests that when curiosity is given time to reflect upon "the self," morally significant lessons can be learned. This resonates with a long tradition in existentialist thought which holds that the self is able to look inward, be curious about itself, and deliberately curate its ethical existence (Augustine, 400/1992; Sartre, 1946/1973).

Reflective away-days are atypical in the dataset. More common means of sparking moral curiosity, and thereby fostering moral development, include: sending weekly voice memos ("I ... call out different virtues and values of who we are" [P16]), surveying employee sentiments ("each month we take a value and ... ask targeted questions around that value" [P22]), and having intentionally small teams (one participant links a "small team mentality" to feeling "aligned" with his values [P1]).

But no means of moral development appears as effective for novices as engaging with exemplars (Zagzebski, 2004; Engelen et al., 2018). Consider the following reflection from a financial broker:

> [The company values are] in the physical space ... I don't ... remember seeing any posters saying, "These are [our] values".... But I guess [they're] just [in] the environment, [in] people's characteristics. [They're] embodied literally ... by people, which is genius. (P2)

What makes this phenomenon akin to "genius," I suggest, has to do with role modeling's mix of passive and active elements. Role models of some sort exist in close proximity to the broker. This is an important start. But, as exemplarist paradigms insist, it is insufficient to merely see people who embody or lead with values. Active elements must also be involved. An emotion (admiration) as well as an action (imitation, perhaps preceded by critical reflection) are engaged upon witnessing exemplary individuals (Algoe and Haidt, 2009; Zagzebski, 2017; Henderson, 2022).

So much is seen in participant responses. "I've stayed [in the bank]," says an account manager, "because I've found people who've *inspired* me ... and allowed me to see how [I] can be the kind of person I am ..., have the level of empathy I have, and ... *use that to help* people within the organization" (P28, emphasis added). Reflecting upon leadership, an alternative-investments analyst echoes the same emotion-to-action sequence: "I will try and engender the things that I *admire* ... I will try and *instill* them in future places" (P33). Thus, the emotion of admiration is seen to involve an impetus or motive to act – specifically to imitate the person admired (Zagzebski, 2003). In this way, admiration serves as a potent psychological mechanism for socially mediated moral learning (Bandura, 1977; Zagzebski, 2013, 2017).

Should moral curiosity be sated predominantly or solely by the example of others? Some would insist not. Sceptics fear the possibility of hero worship – involving the uncritical imitation of a model's less admirable traits (Szutta, 2019). Others simply point to alternative and possibly more effective means of moral learning. Kristjánsson (2017), for instance, encourages a Platonic approach – learning from the purity of "transpersonal moral ideals" (p. 32) rather than the messy example of role models. How might novices respond? To the charge of hero worship, novices appear to avoid its temptations through an innate sense of integrity (I discuss this point in Section 3.3). To the proposal concerning transpersonal moral ideals, novices themselves speak against this. Indeed, if we understand company values to be a corporate equivalent of transpersonal moral ideals, then it appears that novices – including the broker above (P2) – eschew approaches to moral learning that predominantly rely upon rational engagement with abstract ideas. As one participant frankly says: "I don't take ... notice of [the company values] at all" (P13).

3.2 Humility Complements Curiosity

Curiosity may be the distinguishing character strength of novices, but, as a wealth-management associate suggests, it is not the only character strength required of new starters. Incensed by the "disrespectful[ness]" of junior colleagues, the associate explains:

> No one owes you anything when you join a bank ... I've seen very disrespectful graduates who just think they're going to be ... senior banker[s] in two years and that's [that]. I hate it. Management hates it. So, being *humble* and being ready to just listen and move forward ... That, I think, is crucial. (P12, emphasis added)

What does "being humble" entail? Chancellor and Lyubomirsky (2013) identify several hallmarks of this underappreciated virtue, which include an accurate perspective of oneself, an openness to new information, as well as an outward and even egalitarian emphasis on others. For the associate, certain colleagues lack these hallmarks in part or altogether. He describes this lacuna as "disrespectful" (P12), but I would name a possible underlying trait: arrogance, a vicious counterpart to humility.

I do not see much discussion of arrogance per se in the data (most likely due to the interview guide's emphasis on positive strengths of character). But the ways in which novices navigate humility and arrogance – thus keeping themselves "equidistant from ... the extremes" (Aristotle, 350 BC/2009, bk. II.6) – can be clearly seen. Take, for instance, the following reflections from a back-office professional at the V-level (just under the C-suite), who describes a difficult transition from a large bank to a small investment firm. Recounting her struggles with the slower pace, she recalls the frustration of her new managers with her then-arrogant behavior:

> [The firm] was like, "Who the hell does she think she is, coming in here and ... poking holes at the way we operate ... and being really aggressive? ... That's not how we run this organization!" But, thankfully, one of the executives ... saw a bit of himself in me and decided to take me under his wing [to] try and coach me through [the transition]. (P19)

This excerpt may speak to the humility of the executive who took the interviewee under his wing (after all, he could have rejected her opinions full stop, thus displaying some degree of arrogance). Yet the use of the word "thankfully" betrays a nascent humility – as well as an overcoming of arrogance – on the interviewee's part. In other words, she is thankful that she was able to receive coaching to exercise an ability to focus on others (apart from herself and her old standards of performance) and thus cultivate what Davis, Worthington, and Hook (2010) describe as "relational humility" (p. 248).

"It was a bit of a journey for me," the back-office professional concludes. But now her values are "more on the people side" (P19). She immediately explains:

> Historically ... people didn't exist in investment banking. You are just a cog and you just move around and you press buttons all day and you can't screw it up. [Now, for me,] it's more about empathy and relationships – not just within the organization but also how we deal with people externally ... Like, you are not just a service provider. We want to create a long-term relationship with you. It's a bit more than just business. (P19)

This back-office story offers a tale of personal transformation involving a struggle with humility's demands and, happily, an acquisition of new ways of thinking. Is curiosity – with its aim of acquiring new information – implicated in her change of attitude? Asserting this link would be a stretch. (Her transformation seemed more like a practical necessity than the result of moral curiosity.) But elsewhere in the data, I find strong connections between humility and the sorts of knowledge that could be associated with curiosity in its moral, self-referential form.

Consider this anecdote – relating to moral know-how and humility – from the wealth manager introduced above. Confronted with an ethically dubious investment decision, he asks himself, "How do I deal with [this]?" The answer, he says, can never be found by "insulat[ing]" the issue (i.e., hiding the situation from others), but rather by "express[ing] it." "We're taught early on," he continues, "[to] go to [our] management teams, those who are more experienced," to find answers (P12). In this account, I see a humble sourcing of new and morally relevant information – a stark contrast to the behaviors of the "very disrespectful graduates" he previously described (P12). Is curiosity here implicated? I think so. Not only does he take the time to ask a question – a characteristic act of curiosity (Watson, 2022) – but he also asserts soon after that he "continue[s] to be inquisitive, ... to ask questions, [and is] never ... afraid to put [his] hand up" (P12). For this novice, humility and curiosity go hand in hand. And this is especially important since novices – as their name suggests, and as the associate admits – characteristically have limited moral experience.

Consider yet another anecdote, one that illustrates the struggle that novices face when confronted by "new insights about themselves and the world" (Chancellor and Lyubomirsky, 2013, p. 825). In this anecdote, an alternative-investments analyst describes her struggle with the perceived immorality of her sector. "When I had a bit of a wobble, about ... [whether alternative investing] was for me, ... [my boss] spent time with me, just talking about what it was I was looking for" (P33). Following that conversation, and equipped with new insights, the analyst goes on to explain her developing thoughts: "[alternative investments] ... [are] inevitably ... profit-driven ... I've been coming to terms with that fact ... It's just different. And I need to accept that and find my sense of purpose and self-worth ... somewhere else in life" (P33).

By "coming to terms" with the sector's profit-driven nature, the analyst displays what Whitcomb et al. (2017) call the "limitation-owning" dimension of humility: She "owns" information that she had previously sought to deny (p. 528). Moreover, one could say that humility helps the analyst "mediate ideas fairly" (Park, Vyver, and Bretherton, 2020, p. 2): She presumably approached this information (regarding the profit-driven nature of alternative investments) in a measured way, despite facing new and even uncomfortable facts (e.g., her need to find purpose elsewhere in life). Someone might argue, of course, that alternative investments are *not* all about profit and that the analyst has not fairly handled, or accurately interpreted, the information received. But one can easily imagine a situation wherein less humble, or arrogant, analysts decide to ignore their "wobble[s]" and not "com[e] to terms with" facts of strong moral significance (P33). Such analysts might blindly drive forwards, "think[ing] they're going to be ... senior banker[s or the equivalent] in two years and that's [that]" (P12). By contrast, the alternative-investments analyst has – at the very least – paused to humbly ask for morally relevant information. Such questioning is an important element of curiosity in its moral form.

3.3 Integrity Helps Curiosity Discern Good from Bad

Novices at any seniority level may carry tremendous weight upon their shoulders. But no burden seems as heavy or important for novices as maintaining their own integrity, especially when exposed to bad role models – in other words, "anti-exemplars" (Robinson, 2016). Consider this reflection from a discerning mid-level engineer:

> I sometimes ... choose to not see people as role models ... I can remember one meeting [where the leaders] ... asked this guy who'd been working ridiculous hours to comment on ... stuff that he was doing. He ... sounded absolutely exhausted. And they were trying to use him ... as ... an example of ... [the] "really fun things" [we can do] ... [Later, I said to my boss,] "If you think that's going to motivate people, that's not going to work. He sounded like he was on death's door." (P8)

Here, the engineer describes a situation wherein an individual was put forth as an exemplary figure, someone whom the leaders think is deserving of admiration and emulation (Zagzebski, 2017). However, something in the engineer stops her from seeing her colleague as a role model. What this might be, I suggest, is integrity.

Positive psychologists understand integrity to be a type of character strength, involving (i) a sense of wholeness, (ii) consistency in word and deed, (iii) authenticity with oneself, and (iv) ethical behavior (Peterson and Seligman, 2004; Palanski and Yammarino, 2007). At the very least, the engineer's remarks imply a concern with *wholeness*: She does not want "ridiculous [work] hours" to take over her or another's life (P8). She also displays a certain *internal consistency*: After telling this story, the engineer shares that she enjoys "raising people up" and thinks that she would not be able to do this were she promoted to a senior role. A directorship, she concludes, "does not look very attractive ... Whether I'm aspiring for that title in particular, I'm not entirely sure" (P8).

Behind this latter conclusion lies a further concern over *authenticity* – or that "grounded feeling," as one associate defines it (P5). Indeed, for the engineer, to be a director is to become someone she does not want to be. And finally, the engineer tacitly links authenticity with *ethical behavior*. As Gentry et al. (2013) note, authenticity entails "*using* ethical considerations to guide decisions and actions" (p. 396, emphasis added). Such considerations are certainly top of mind for this participant: For her, to let someone linger at "death's door" – and to be proud or aloof about it – is ethically questionable (P8).

Integrity's link with the *use* of ethical considerations is elsewhere reflected in the interview data. Consider the following remarks from two junior professionals (respectively, the wealth-management and the investment associates encountered above):

> I'm quite a stickler for integrity. So, what does this mean for me? It means that, in anything I do, whether someone is looking or not, ... [I do] the right thing. I try to live by that rule. I think it helps me in my personal life, my professional life. Whenever I make an action or decision, I think: "Is this the right thing to do?" (P12)

> I've ... seen [my boss] ... forego an economic benefit in order to maintain integrity ... It's usually the grey areas where you see these virtues come out. In this case, there was nothing illegal ... It was just a moral question. "What kind of person do you want to be known for?" ... He's taken that high-integrity route. (P29)

Both excerpts point to distinct uses of ethical information. In speaking of himself, the wealth manager defines integrity as a rule that helps him do "the right thing"

(P12). In contrast, the investment associate links integrity with virtues that pertain to the "kind of person" the moral agent "want[s] to be" (P29). While it may be tempting to view these excerpts as representing incompatible moral approaches (deontology *versus* virtue ethics), it is more fruitful to focus on what they have in common. This commonality, I suggest, has to do with integrity's link to practical wisdom (Roca, 2008) – the master virtue that helps individuals deliberate well about "what is good and expedient" for themselves and about the "sorts of thing conducive to the good life in general" (Aristotle, 350 BC/2009, bk. VI.5).

Scholars have long associated integrity with this master virtue. Werpehowski (2007) refers to integrity as "a kind of self-renewing perseverance" (p. 56), pertaining to the development of an individual's "practical [moral] wisdom" (p. 67). And Palanski and Yammarino (2007) link integrity with moral wholeness, which involves "being true to oneself and moral/ethical behavior" (p. 173). Both understandings – insofar as they associate integrity with moral reasoning and truth – resonate with the definition of practical wisdom (or prudence) offered by Saint Thomas Aquinas (1266/1964): "it belongs to prudence [i.e., practical wisdom] ... to apply right reason to action" (pt. II-II, q. 47, a. 4) and, specifically, to apply "universal principles to the particular[ities ...] of practical matters" (pt. II-II, q. 47, a. 6).

Considered together, the two excerpts above– from the rule-following associate and his virtue-guided counterpart – track closely the relationship between integrity and practical wisdom. To have integrity is to be guided rightly in one's moral reasoning; and to be guided rightly is to have practical wisdom. It is no surprise, then, that novices – who display moral curiosity to an admirable degree – resonate with questions, such as "Is this the right thing to do?" (P12) or "What kind of person do you want to be known for?" (P29). Such questions speak to a budding form of practical wisdom and, in particular, to the integrity that novices use to critically navigate familiar and newly acquired moral information. With any morally relevant information, novices ask whether the content is right for them ("I sometimes ... choose to not see people as role models" [P8]), right for others (Is it "raising people up"? [P8]), or right in general ("Is this the right thing to do?" [P12]). Integrity thus serves as an important complement – a guiding virtue – for novices in finance. As they lead themselves or others, it guides their moral questioning.

3.4 Summary and Discussion: Novices as Self Leaders

Let us take stock. Presented by subtheme, my account of the novice-type suggests that:

1. *The curious prefer learning from exemplars.* Novices are distinguished for their curiosity (Watson, 2022), which serves as a "mainspring of motivation"

(Miscevic, 2007, p. 246) not only for professional achievements but also for moral development. No means of sparking moral curiosity is as effective for novices as engaging with exemplars. Exemplarist moral learning engages the emotion of admiration, ideally involves critical reflection, and culminates in the characteristic act of imitation (Zagzebski, 2013, 2017). Moral learning from company values, a corporate manifestation of "transpersonal moral ideals" (Kristjánsson, 2017, p. 32), is not preferred by novices in the dataset. Novices avoid hero worship by evaluating possible exemplars against their own moral standards.

2. *Humility complements curiosity.* Novices are both curious and humble. Humility entails an accurate perspective of oneself, an openness to new information, and an outward, even egalitarian, emphasis on others (Chancellor and Lyubomirsky, 2013). "Relational humility" helps novices handle job situations in which their own pride or arrogance might get in the way (Davis, Worthington, and Hook, 2010, p. 248). The humility of novices helps them source important types of ethical information, including moral know-how (knowledge of how to handle a difficult situation) and personal moral insight (knowledge of their own struggles, doubts, and moral convictions). Due to its role in sourcing new information, humility is an important complement to curiosity. One might even say that it is a prerequisite virtue to curiosity.

3. *Integrity helps curiosity discern good from bad.* Novices resist imitating anti-exemplars (Robinson, 2016) by exercising their integrity. Integrity involves a sense of wholeness, consistency in word and deed, authenticity with oneself, and ethical behavior (Peterson and Seligman, 2004; Palanski and Yammarino, 2007). The ethical behavior of novices shows evidence of deontological and virtue-ethical sources. Whatever their preferred moral tradition, novices display practical wisdom through their application of ethical principles to specific situations (Aquinas, 1266/1964), including their assessment of supposed leadership exemplars. The exercise of practical wisdom thus contributes to the integrity of novices (Werpehowski, 2007). And questioning – involving an asking for and an openness to morally relevant information (Maile, 2024) – supports their integrity.

A chief analytical claim of this Element is that novices – along with heroes and sages – highlight different ways in which "leading by example" works, particularly with respect to admiration and various responses to this imitative emotion. In this section, I suggested that novices underscore a fundamental aspect of leading by example: its reliance upon admiration. Novices especially showcase this aspect because, among the interviewees, it is the morally curious who consistently speak in exemplarist terms: "I will try and engender the things that I admire" (P33), "[Our] values .... [are] embodied literally ... by people, which is genius" (P2). These are but two occasions of novices using exemplarist speech, while gesturing toward the admirable in the role-modeling process. My analysis thus corroborates exemplarist positions – especially those of Zagzebski (2003, 2013), but also of Algoe and Haidt (2009) – which hold that admiration is morally motivating (it helps initiate exemplarist moral learning) and has imitation as a characteristic act (learners who experience admiration typically, though not always, seek to imitate their exemplar in some respect).

The significance of this finding has to do with the state of current research. As I suggest in Section 2.1, research in positive leadership could benefit from an "emotional sensitization" (Kristjánsson, 2017, p. 21). Admiration – especially Zagzebski's conception of it – is intensely debated in education contexts (Szutta, 2019; Watson, 2019), but investigation of it in the workplace, including the financial workplace, is lacking. My analysis helps advance exemplarist investigation in this important sphere. At the very least, it finds admiration in a morally contested sector: Popular opinion notwithstanding, admiration of moral figures *does* exist in finance.

More significantly, my analysis suggests that admiration – including the role-modeling process it initiates – should be subject to the demands of moral curiosity. If novices are to be admired (and thus influence the "central terms" of our "moral discourse" [Zagzebski, 2017]), then finance professionals may learn from them the vital art of questioning. Novices do not blindly follow where their admiration leads: They take time to ask morally salient questions about the exemplary figures they encounter.

Their questions, moreover, are shaped by practical wisdom's self- and other-regarding concern. Zagzebski (2017) associates one's internal criticism, or testing, of admiration with the notion of "conscientious self-reflection": We trust admiration if "it survives reflection over time" (p. 45). But novices might add that admiration is to be trusted if it survives *moral questioning* over time: Does a given experience of admiration point to "the right thing to do" (P12)? Does it align with the "kind of person ... [I] want to be known for" (P29)? Moral questioning and self-reflection are not mutually exclusive, of course. Yet the former is to be embraced because it adds useful, practical specificity to the latter. To improve in self-reflection, one should ask moral questions – not only about what's good for oneself but also about what's good for others. This is an important lesson about admiration – and about being an exemplary leader in general – that the novice-type draws out.

I conclude this section by mentioning just one area of research in which our knowledge of novices – and of leading by example – may be extended. Of course, there are many areas regarding, for instance, the types of questions novices ask (Do they ask open or closed questions?), the social conditions of their questioning (Do they build rapport with their respondent?), how they came to be curious in the first place (Were they curious from childhood or more recently on the job?), or how successful their questioning might be (Does their questioning result in lasting characterological change?). But given my claim that novices are leaders in their own right, I would like to address their specific type of leadership as understood in relation to their distinct domain of leading by example.

Whether at the beginning of their careers or established in the C-suite, novices constitute a discernible type of positive leader. The domain in which they excel most may be called *self-leadership*, which, as Neck and Houghton (2006) propose, involves "specific behavioral and cognitive strategies designed to positively influence personal effectiveness" (p. 271). Previous research on self-leadership endorses strategies such as heightening one's self-awareness during unpleasant but necessary tasks, or mentally congratulating oneself when self-set goals are achieved (Neck and Manz, 2013). These strategies are undoubtedly important for professional and personal, moral development. But, as my portrait of the novice suggests, self-leadership may also be supported by attention to workplace exemplars.

Future research in self-leadership could draw attention to the emotion of admiration and the role it plays in developing one's "personal effectiveness" (Neck and Houghton, 2006). My analysis shows that novices are generally motivated to follow the example of admirable individuals. Further empirical research could explore causal or correlative links between specific occasions of admiration and particular instances of, or intentions for, self-leading. Algoe and Haidt (2009) do something similar. Using videos to induce admiration in research participants, they found a positive link between admiration and motives to improve in a skill or talent. Their study could be tweaked to focus on specific aspects of self-leadership as defined, for instance, by Neck and Manz (2013) or as relevant for different finance leaders.

This sort of study might also be triangulated with results from a brief implicit association test (Sriram and Greenwald, 2009), which could corroborate, or challenge, the claim advanced here that particular strengths of character – curiosity, humility, and integrity – are associated with successful self-leadership efforts. Maybe employees can successfully lead themselves without being curious, humble, or possessing integrity. And maybe they can lead without learning from admirable figures. These are worthy hypotheses to empirically test. But, from an LBE perspective, I suspect that self-leadership is made difficult without the prerequisite virtues that the novice-type exemplifies.

4 Heroes Connect Empathy to Admiration

My analysis now moves to a second theme: the *hero* exemplar-type. In classic literatures, the typical hero shows exceptional courage in war (Luo, 2004; Virgil, 2007). In finance, the hero displays courage as well, but does so in a very different context: an emotionally "fraught" banking environment (P6). Because of this, the sector's hero requires an additional and arguably more relevant strength of character – namely, "empathy" which participants explicitly associate with "feeling[s]" (P28), "relationships" (P19), "encourage[ment]" (P9), and "emotional intelligence" (P24, P12, P11). In the dataset, a link between courage and empathy is strongly suggested. Describing her approach to leadership, a back-office professional describes courage in terms of a vulnerable, self-sacrificial support of her team: "I've stuck my neck out and I've shown courage ... [This involves] self-sacrifice and genuinely caring for people" (P19). Reflecting on his personal strengths of character, a client manager makes a similar connection: "[I] need to be comfortable operating with uncertainty ... I've got to involve stakeholders that ... [may be] unhappy ... So, [I] need a bit of courage. [I] need to be prepared to stick [my] head above the parapet" (P17). And a senior banker includes "courage" in her list of core virtues that constitute her "collaborative and open" style of team leadership that, she adds, features a "pretty good" amount of "emotional intelligence" (P11).

In this section, I focus upon the empathic side of the connection made between courage and empathy. This emphasis elucidates what courage can look like in the financial workplace. It also sheds light on empathy as a core virtue of heroic team leadership: As a wealth-management associate says, his workplace "hero" takes time to "listen" and, like a good military general, stays in the "trenches" with his team (P12). Investigation of a heroic form of leadership – specifically, a heroic form of empathy – can help us understand what makes heroes in finance so admirable in their teams' eyes. In turn, such investigation can help us appreciate LBE from another invaluable perspective.

With regard to my theoretical explorations, the central claim of this section is as follows: that the hero exemplar-type underscores the importance of empathy for leading by example, particularly in team settings. I substantiate this claim through three subthemes or propositions. The first proposition has to do with the specific environment in which heroes operate. Simply put, finance demands empathy. The sector features emotional highs and lows, and this sets the tone for what is expected of team leaders: Heroes must deal with, not ignore, these emotions (Section 4.1). The second proposition concerns empathy itself. In contrast to technical definitions of empathy (which focus on empathy's ability to perceive others' emotions and perspectives), participants' understanding of empathy is explicitly prosocial. For them, empathy always terminates in caring support (Section 4.2). Finally, my third proposition pertains to a specific consequence of heroic empathy. In the dataset, empathy is rewarded with admiration, and admiration begets more empathy from the heroic leader. I refer to this phenomenon as the empathy–admiration loop, and I suggest that it is a basic feature not only of the hero exemplar-type but also of successful attempts to lead by example (Section 4.3). I close this section by summarizing my propositions and elaborating upon the notion that heroes are exemplary team leaders (Section 4.4).

4.1 Finance Demands Empathy

Participants in the dataset offer rich definitions of empathy, describing it in terms of "feeling[s]" (P28), "relationships" (P19), and "emotional intelligence" (P11). I have already noted the connection that participants make between empathy and courage. I now highlight an additional association made: the link between (i) empathy and (ii) participants' normative assessments of finance which, by participants' lights, is a sector that demands empathic team behaviors. Exploration of this link does two things. First, it provides context for participants' understanding of empathy: It is a decidedly team-oriented virtue. Second, it offers a pointedly affective characterization of the sector, one that accounts for negative as well as positive emotions. With the latter often overlooked in popular accounts of the sector (Kay, 2015; Lewis, 2015), it is no surprise that admiration and positive leadership are under-researched in finance.

So, what do participants say about a sector that – in the opinion of many – requires a human touch, one that empathy is seen to provide? The most prominent description centers on human emotion. A senior trader describes "the banking environment" as "fraught," where "time can be short" and "people can have a bit of a temper." Amid these "problems," he continues, one has to "recogniz[e] that there will be emotions ... and [thus one has to] not ... take things personally, but allow th[e] emotion[s of others] to be expressed" (P6). Focusing on his own emotions instead, an executive at an investment firm stresses a "decoupling of the ego from ... assets": "if you're constantly moved by price – price is high today, I feel great; price is low today, I feel terrible – then you're on [an] emotional roller coaster which is incredibly difficult" to manage (P16).

The underlying substance of these reflections is not new. Emotions have featured in modern economic thinking since the eighteenth century, with Adam Smith (1776/2008) describing the effects of human desires upon economic decision-making. More recently emotions in the boardroom, particularly in light of the global financial crisis, have caught the attention of researchers and pundits alike (McKay, Adam, dir. 2015. *The Big Short*. Paramount Pictures).

Thus, what is notable in these reflections pertains to the *positive* manner with which emotions should be dealt – even at the expense of a bank's financial performance. As the senior trader continues to say, "recognizing ... emotions ... and [thus] keep[ing] the peace ... [may] not necessarily [be] the right thing for the bank longer term"; but it is a good way to help colleagues "do more ... to perhaps propagate or help their growth" (P6). The trader's claim certainly begs many questions. For instance, how exactly does attending to colleagues' emotions undermine long-term financial performance? Unable to address this question here, I instead point to the dichotomy implied in the trader's claim, one that positions people (colleagues) *against* numbers (financial performance).

This dichotomy is challenged by a second and aspirational description of the sector: the notion that finance values people *and* numbers. This description is variously expressed in the dataset. Reflecting upon the virtues needed for her investment role, an associate highlights the importance of technical ability, but concludes that empathy toward colleagues is more fundamental: "You have to ... [be good at] the numerical analysis," she says. "But I don't think that's necessarily how you speak to other people ... Empathy ... [is what] I see in my day-to-day which goes above the numerical" (P30). Similarly, a director at a retail bank says she had once thought that "banking was all about maths." But "actually it's not," she says, "... it's more [about] people" (P26). These reflections evince both description and moral aspiration: The participants describe what they see in their daily work experience; but, as Boje (1991) might say, they also remind themselves of an ideal institutional story – what work ought to look like when done well. At minimum, the financial workplace requires attention to people and numbers. At its most aspirational, it "goes above the numerical" (P30): It values people (colleagues) *over* numbers (financial performance).

Whatever the degree of aspiration, virtually all participants describe circumstances at work in which a relationship between people and numbers must be navigated with care. These kinds of situation surely test heroic empathy. Consider two extended examples.

First, the investment associate above recounts "individuals who will scream at people across the office floor, and no one will say a thing" (P30). How does this happen in a company that prides itself on "a very collaborative work environment"? For one, she says, the company values are lived out "in theory," not in practice. This results from a "dated banking environment" where the "hierarchical nature of everything" allows some "superiors" to adopt an "attitude ... [of] 'you can't make mistakes.'" In effect, they "value those [aggressive] behaviors," which ultimately "work well [for] clients," but not for teammates. Moreover, she says, "I am 100% sure [that] . . . our management team . . . would never encounter someone speaking to [or yelling at] them [in] this way." They simply "wouldn't witness it" because, in her opinion, their approach to solving these issues is not empathetic: It does not come "from the bottom up"; they are not with the people, "bringing people in" (P30).

Next, consider this common challenge involving people and numbers at a large bank. There's a "constant threat over most people's heads that there could be a restructure," says a senior manager, ". . . [that] you could lose your job year-to-year" (P7). No surprise, then, that "fear" exists in the organization: This is "the bit that . . . we still haven't quite got right." Nevertheless, to save the bank, the manager recognizes that cuts must be made, and he admits that he usually holds the axe. How does he handle the pressure? "You've got to think . . .," he says,

> to enable the organization to survive, you have to get rid of people that are not performing . . . You've got to switch off some of your emotions . . . and just . . . bring out the banker, dial down the human. (P7)

These stories add to a growing list of well-documented behaviors and less-than-optimal working conditions in the financial services. Lee and Kim (2021) describe verbal violence in banking, identifying psychological exhaustion as a significant consequence. The academic literature is awash with studies concerning the people-challenges experienced by management (Frohman and Johnson, 1993; Osterman, 2008; Gjerde and Alvesson, 2020; Reynders, Kumar, and Found, 2022). And investigative journalist Joris Luyendijk (2013, 2015), like the senior manager above, highlights how bankers face looming threats of job termination, particularly in sub-industries that may be especially prone to workforce contraction. Empathy, I suggest, is implicated in all these scenarios. And *how* it is manifested will look quite different, depending on circumstance and the exact type or dimension of empathy involved. So, handling people and numbers with care *is* possible. Determining how to do this is the hero's task.

4.2 Empathy Has Three Acts

"[T]he heroes in the industry . . . succeed commercially," says an investment executive, and they align with "what's good . . . for humankind." They may "be a bit of a dick sometimes," but their typical behaviors are "not . . . mutually exclusive" (P31). As implied by the executive, the sector's heroes are not saints: They are far from perfect. Nevertheless, they are admired. The reason for this has to do with their empathic behavior. But what does it mean to be empathic toward others, specifically to colleagues in the financial workplace?

One participant, an account manager, offers a detailed explanation. When asked to define empathy (the participant's self-identified core virtue), she does so by contrasting it with sympathy. "Sympathy," she explains, "is listening to somebody on a surface level [and] offering support." On the other hand,

> empathy is trying to *understand* ... what they might be feeling. [You are] therefore *offering support* from a position of either ... understand[ing] what [they] are feeling, or a position of honesty – [that] is, [admitting that you] really can't understand what [they] are feeling, so [they need] to talk ..., [to] tell [you] how it is. (P28, emphasis added)

The participant's explanation resonates with central features of empathy as expressed by interviewees across the dataset: consider, for instance, a shared emphasis upon "emotional aware[ness]" (P11) and being "supportive" of others (P8). Notably, the participant's explanation also resonates with certain technical understandings of empathy – specifically those that describe empathy as "other-focused" and involving "a willingness to help or protect the target" (Duan and Sager, 2016, pp. 535–536). Understood as a prosocial disposition (Duan and Hill, 1996), empathy of this stripe may usefully be called "empathic concern" (Duan and Sager, 2016, p. 535), which distinguishes it from more simplistic and less positive notions that focus exclusively on an ability to feel another's emotions. As Darwall (1998) notes, empathy of this latter kind "can be consistent with the indifference of pure observation or even the cruelty of sadism" (p. 261). For present purposes, I will continue to define empathy according to the prosocial understanding of interviewees.

Let us return, then, to the account manager introduced above (P28). Her description of empathy outlines three distinct steps: listening, understanding, and offering support. These steps align with the influential perception–action model of empathy as detailed by Preston and de Waal (2002). As I read it, this neurological view holds that empathy has three stages. To start, empathy (i) perceives another person's emotions, involving an "emotional contagion" of that person's affective state (Preston and de Waal, 2002, p. 2). Next, it (ii) seeks to understand that person's perspective, relying on different informational sources, including data supplied by the preceding emotional contagion and the empathizer's own preexisting representations of emotions and experiences (Preston and de Waal, 2002, p. 5; Preston, 2007, pp. 428–433). Finally, empathy (iii) culminates in spontaneous bodily responses from the empathizer, for example, a mirrored frown, and – at its moral best – it results in prosocial "helping behavior" (Preston and de Waal, 2002, p. 4). This view assumes that empathy has an intrinsic moral dimension – or what Hildebrand (2023) might call "internal resources necessary to guide moral action," such as deontic principles (fn. 37 on p. 1001) – but unfortunately, though perhaps unsurprisingly, the account manager does not articulate what empathy's inner morality might be.

Setting aside the question of normative sources for the time being, allow me to focus on empathy's three stages as presented elsewhere in the dataset. Take, for instance, a broker's description of empathy (notably used in a client-facing, not colleague-related, context): "empathy," he says, "is connecting with the customer ... For me, [it] means *understanding* and just *listening* to that person and caring about what they've just told you. You know, like *genuinely caring*" (P2, emphasis added). Or consider this extended reflection from a senior banker concerning remote work during the pandemic: with "more people working from home, ... [we] are at the point of burnout," she says (P11). The bank tries "to encourage [colleagues] ... to take leave and be aware of their own wellbeing"; it offers professional counseling services so that people can talk about "challenging topics." But, given "the storm" everyone is in, the banker takes it upon herself to offer a more personal and empathic approach, especially when it comes to overburdened workloads. "We can't do everything," she admits,

> [so, I have] regular stand-ups ... to re-prioritize and de-prioritize [people's work], ... we communicate more, ... [and] I always say this to ... my team: "We're not doing open heart surgery. This is not life or death. This is financial services. We have a mandate. Let's deliver ... [but] let's still have a bit of fun." (P11)

In psychological studies, empathic behaviors – like those of the banker – are usually observed in circumstances of acute distress (Preston, 2016). In fact, as Duan and Sager (2016) note, for evolutionary reasons, it is neurologically harder for humans to share joy than feelings of distress: Empathy with the latter is, and has been, more highly socially rewarded. In the above reflection, this pattern continues. Amid the distress of the pandemic, the senior banker displays (i) empathic listening in her awareness of colleague "burnout," (ii) empathic understanding through her "regular stand-ups," and (iii) empathic support in her decision to "stay close" to her team (P11). Aware of the bank's professional counseling services, she goes above and beyond the institutional response. Such is the heroism of the sector's empaths – and, indeed, it does not go unnoticed.

4.3 Empathy Elicits Admiration

My analysis thus far shows that participants largely understand empathy according to its prosocial variant. But the data suggest that there is more to interviewees' understanding than meets the eye. Since participants discuss empathy in terms of exemplary others (including their own exemplary selves), they appear to implicate empathy in what it means to lead by example. In doing so, they draw together empathy (involving an ability to feel another's emotions) and admiration (the central emotion of leading by example). Two points are worth drawing out.

The first pertains to the emotion of admiration. Empathy appears to generate admiration in those who witness or benefit from a hero's empathic behavior. An alternative-investments analyst, for instance, says that she "admires" her boss who took a chance in giving her a job: He shared a similar background with her and "understood where [she] was coming from." "He felt like a good guy," she says (P33). And many other participants suggest that admiration is or has been elicited in their imitation of empathic leaders. For example, a senior financial controller associates her "very empathetic approach to leadership" with an empathic executive for whom she has "an enormous amount of respect" (P9); an investment associate says he was "really attracted" by the reputation of his firm's "empath[etic] ... servant leaders" (P29); and an account manager considers her bank's CEO to be an empathic individual, someone who models for her how to use "empathy ... at the right time" (P28).

The fact that empathy elicits admiration is not significant in itself: After all, *any* virtue will elicit admiration in theory. Instead, the significance here involves the confluence of two phenomena: First, the fact that empathy, by definition, entails the ability to feel another's emotions; and, second, the fact that admiration – specifically the admiration that others hold toward an empath – can be one of the emotions that an empath feels. In a role-modeling context, the coming together of these phenomena suggests that finance's heroes are especially good at modeling ethical behaviors *precisely* because they are good at (i) perceiving the admiration that is directed toward them (more so than, say, a stereotypically courageous exemplar whose signal virtue does not necessarily involve the ability to feel others' emotions) and (ii) supporting the person who admires them (since such support is characteristic of their prosocial empathy).

The second point I wish to make, then, is this: that empathy appears to strengthen leaders' ability to be, or to remain, exemplary by informing them of the admiration that their virtuous acts generate. This emotional information (Zagzebski, 2003) – which in theory is felt at a deeply affective level and which acts as a form of social reward (Duan and Sager, 2016) – helps motivate leaders to continue in their virtuous ways. I refer to this phenomenon as the *empathy–admiration loop*. I think that it applies to empathic leaders especially, but I suspect that it can be associated with any exemplar who exercises empathy in the way indicated in this section.

Consider this anecdote involving empathy and admiration, described in the context of team leadership and career progression. A finance director says this of herself:

> Empathy is something that ... has taken me to the level I am now. It helps me to relate with my team and make[s] them ... perform to the level that I want [them] to perform. (P20)

She explains: "I am not just managing ... project[s], I am there working with everyone ... listening to exactly what is going on and understanding the details of their comments." Doing this helps her teammates to grow, to "push themselves" in personal and professional development. Feeling "appreciate[d]" – or admired – by them, she is inspired to continue these empathic behaviors: "I do care about my team, quite a lot," she claims (P20).

While reading her account, one may question whether the director's teammates actually admire her. Some readers might think her behaviors evince micromanagement, and many would agree that micro-managers are not to be admired. But the question of whether the director is actually admired can, for our purposes, be rephrased. I ask instead whether a semblance of admiration – or a subjective representation of it – might inspire her continued empathic behavior. In theory, it could. As neurological studies suggest, it is sufficient for a subject (or empath) to have, in her "brain and body," a "representation" of admiration that is "*similar to* that of the object" – here, the admiration of a teammate (Preston, 2007, p. 430, emphasis in original). In other words, complete accuracy about what others are feeling is not a necessary condition for empathy (Maibom, 2022, chapter 6). The director merely needs some evidence – *some* mark of being "appreciate[d]" (P20) – to support her tacit belief that she is admired and to support her explicit claim that her empathic behaviors are appreciated. Whatever the case, self-narratives like hers are strongly suggestive of a link between empathy, admiration, and continued empathic behavior.

Another anecdote is worth discussing at some length. An executive at an investment firm describes his successful handling of emotions during tense business negotiations. He says the following with cool confidence:

> I tend to be unmoved by emotions ... It's not to say I lack empathy, but ... I tend to be quite ... level-headed .... People's emotional make-up is a huge proportion of any business dealing ... [Nevertheless,] I ... com[e] into negotiations being unoffendable, being willing to tell the truth, ... and hold [the] line. (P16)

While these remarks mention empathy, it is not unreasonable to ask whether the executive really displays empathy in the situation described. As with many queries, the answer depends on the definition used. The account manager above (P28) gives the common prosocial definition. But other understandings, or other aspects of the same definition, exist. Indeed, research confirms that empathy has two dimensions: one cognitive, one affective. Empirical studies typically focus on one of these dimensions and thus leave unanswered the question of how individuals use both to inform their actions (Hoffman, 1984; Mill, 1984; Duan and Hill, 1996). According to Duan and Sager (2016), more contextual studies are needed.

Here, in the executive's context, it appears that the cognitive domain has strong control over an affective reflex – an "emotional contagion" (Duan and Hill, 1996, p. 263) – which, if left unchecked, could cause the executive to lose his "level-headed[ness]" (perhaps mirroring his agitated counterparty) or cause him to not "tell the truth" (by inaccurately interpreting his own or his counterparty's perspectives) (P16).

One might object to my interpretation, however, claiming that the executive either lacks empathy in this instance or that a different strength of character is at play, for example, temperance in his emotions. But empathy research suggests otherwise. At work in the executive may be: (i) "cognitive empathy," which allows the executive to manage his affective representations through a top-down, rational process; (ii) "empathic accuracy," which allows the executive to correctly identify the emotional state and, perhaps by extension, the underlying financial circumstance of the other; or (iii) "true empathy," a form of empathic concern that allows the executive to make a clear distinction between himself and the counterparty, thus avoiding a debilitating emotional conflation with the latter (Preston, 2016, p. 758). In the executive's story, the precise form of empathy, as well as the nature of the relation between the affective and cognitive spheres, is inexact. Nevertheless, it may be safe to conclude that empathy's cognitive dimension features strongly in his negotiating, giving the executive a competitive advantage – a "hold[ing of the] line" – when confronted by a counterparty's "emotional make-up" (P16).

Does the executive's use of empathy elicit admiration? It seems so. Interviewees from the same firm associate the executive's business acumen with the company's success. In the words of one participant, the firm is "phenomenally successful" because of "impressive" colleagues like him (P3). Moreover, one of the other executives – who stresses his "uncompromising" approach to business and morals (perhaps mirroring the first executive's "unmoved ... emotions" [P16]) – speaks candidly about his affection for his colleagues: "I love my team, ... I love my firm," he says (P25).

Admittedly, these are tacit gestures toward admiration, but in a small firm they hold great weight. Perhaps such feelings help explain the first executive's oath to "lay [him]self down on the anvil," facing "pressure and complexity," to serve his team and their mission (P16). I doubt such heroic sentiments, if communicated to colleagues, would fail to elicit some level of admiration.

I doubt, too, that the executive would fail to grow in virtue – empathy included – in response to this admiration. "Has working at your company shaped you as a person?," the interviewer asks. "Without a doubt," he says. "[Like] iron, [and] as one man sharpens the other, it's impossible to be around virtue-seeking people ... and not be challenged" or changed (P16).

4.4 Summary and Discussion: Heroes as Team Leaders

We now take stock. Presented by subtheme, my account of finance's hero suggests that:

1. *Finance demands empathy.* Not unlike popular pundits (Luyendijk, 2015; *The Big Short*, 2018), participants describe the morality of the sector in various, often conflicting, ways. Finance is seen to pit people (especially colleagues) *against* numbers, to value colleagues *and* numbers, or to place colleagues *over* numbers. Whatever their assessment, participants note the emotional roller coaster that they constantly face. To deal with this, participants expect emotional intelligence and support from their leaders. Thus, empathy emerges as a necessary strength of character for team leadership in the sector.
2. *Empathy has three acts.* According to participants, empathy has a prosocial and caring dimension (Duan and Sager, 2016). Participants thus move away from a narrow and morally neutral understanding that stresses empathy's ability to merely perceive others' emotions (Preston, 2016). Notably, Preston and de Waal's (2002) perception–action model of empathy can be discerned in the data. Participants suggest that empathy (i) perceives another person's emotions through emotional contagion; (ii) understands the person's perspectives based on felt emotions, past experiences, and related representations; and (iii) culminates in spontaneous bodily responses, for example, a mirrored frown, and, as an additional outcome, decidedly moral behavior (Hildebrand, 2023).
3. *Empathy elicits admiration.* Empathic leaders go out of their way to provide colleagues with moral support, and this effort does not go unrewarded. In the data, it appears that empathic behavior is rewarded by increased admiration of the empathizers. And since empaths are especially good at perceiving others' emotions (Preston, 2007), including the emotions of those whom they support, they feel the admiration that colleagues direct toward them – which, in turn, motivates empaths to continue in their empathic ways (Zagzebski, 2003). This phenomenon, the empathy–admiration loop, can be found in the successful handling of distressing situations (Preston, 2016; Maibom, 2022), including high-stress work situations and business negotiating.

In this section of the Element, I suggested that the hero exemplar-type uncovers an important link between empathy and leading by example. In particular, I proposed that empathy elicits admiration in those whom empaths support and that empaths' perception of such admiration motivates them to continue in virtue. I refer to this phenomenon as the empathy–admiration loop, and I think it applies to any type of exemplar that displays a prosocial form of empathy. Assuming some truth to these claims, I think the hero-exemplar – including the connection between empathy and admiration – tells us that leading by example is strengthened by the empathic abilities of exemplars themselves: Empathic leaders feel the admiration directed toward them; in response, they continue to act virtuously – partly to live up to social expectations. There is more to say about the empathy–admiration loop, especially in the context of team leadership, but first allow me to address a brief point concerning gender and my conceptualization of the hero-type.

The observant reader may have noticed the many female voices associated with the heroic empath. The stereotype that women have a greater capacity than men to feel and understand others' emotions is well-known (Klein and Hodges, 2001), and empirical research corroborates this belief (Macaskill, Maltby, and Day, 2002; Toussaint and Webb, 2005). My analysis is consistent with these findings. That said, it is important to keep in mind methodological differences: Unlike the quantitative research just cited, my study's thematic analysis does not demand that the researcher follow statistically significant trends in the data – indeed, I do not attempt to find such trends (Braun and Clarke, 2006). Nevertheless, my analysis was guided by participant voices, and empathy was more richly described by women than by men.

Would my analysis have featured a different virtue if there had been fewer female interviewees? Perhaps. But, in current industry contexts, empathy is not described as an explicitly gendered phenomenon, at least not by business entities themselves. It appears that differences in generational expectations, pandemic-related concerns, and the rise of artificial intelligence have contributed to the popularity of empathy – especially its emphasis on the importance of *human* emotion – in industry discourse (Sanchez, 2018; Businessolver, 2022; McKinsey & Company, 2023). It is highly likely that participants in the dataset were familiar with this discourse and, regardless of their gender, made empathy their own. Of course, if there had been more male interviewees than female, it is possible that empathy would have been differently described: While the male broker (P2) describes empathy in a similar way to the female account manager (P28), the male investment executive (P16) appears to exercise a different form of empathy – one that is strongly cognitive and perhaps less obviously prosocial or caring. This possibility, however, does not discredit my analysis of the *available* data.

I return now to the phenomenon of team leadership. In my analysis, I suggested that heroes in finance are exemplary *team* leaders. I made another claim, as well, concerning the empathy–admiration loop: Empathy elicits admiration, and admiration generates more empathy. I think both claims have an obvious relationship: Team leaders grow into their roles in part by enjoying the fruits – including the admiration received from others – of their empathic behaviors. Let me elaborate upon this set of claims to tease out its significance.

First, it is worth reiterating the affective plane on which heroic leadership operates: Heroes in the dataset succeed in managing their own and others' emotions, specifically in a "fraught" industry environment (P6). Heroic team leadership is thus forged on the anvil of negative emotions. Given this context, it is no surprise that participants' heroes display a prosocial form of empathy – one that allows empaths to deal positively with negative emotions.

A related point follows: Heroes in the dataset are often direct line managers or individuals with whom an interviewee has regular, personal contact. This point suggests that heroic leaders are found in the "trenches" (P12). Indeed, the nature of empathy seems to require this. As Preston (2007) notes, empathy "evolved to handle live interactions with other individuals and so live objects [i.e., persons with whom an empath interacts] drive the [empathic] system better than imagined objects, resulting in more intense forms of empathy" (p. 429). In theory, role models do not need to know, or have a relationship with, the individuals who admire them (Moberg, 2000, 2008). But, in finance, it is typical that heroes – *as* role models – know the persons who admire them: It is those same persons that receive heroes' empathic support. This is certainly not always the case – it is safe to assume, for instance, that the account manager is not known by the CEO whom she admires (P28) – but it is common enough in the data to warrant analytical attention.

Such attention speaks to the significance of the hero-type for understanding the "how" of leading by example in UK finance. Of the three types of leaders discussed in this Element, it is the sector's heroes who – by virtue of their empathy and proximity to those they support – appear self-conscious of the admiration directed toward them. This awareness helps motivate heroes to continue "having empathy and caring about the ... broader team, putting them above" the heroes themselves (P29). (Indeed, there appears to be a risk that – without some kind of reward – heroes might give up their empathic behavior: As an investment associate laments, "it's quite exhausting" being empathic all the time, especially "if everyone else [does] not exercise it" [P30].)

Thus, institutional support of exemplary leaders should include a distinctly moral incentive – namely, admiration. Speaking around this point, Algoe and Haidt (2009) quote Thomas Jefferson, the third president of the United States, who said:

> When any ... act of charity or of gratitude, for instance, is presented either to our sight or imagination, we are deeply impressed with its beauty and feel a strong desire in ourselves of doing charitable and grateful acts also. (quoted on p. 106; Jefferson, 1771/1975)

In other words, a good incentive leverages admiration – a strongly imitative emotion – to inspire desirable moral behaviors. Should firms focus exclusively on external incentives, such as commercial rewards or the supposedly "fun things" an employee can do if they never rest (P8), they lessen their chances of developing moral exemplars of any sort – whether heroic empaths, curious novices, or role models of a different sort.

So, who within a firm is responsible for designing proper moral incentives – that is, incentives that elicit and multiply the effects of admiration? Nothing in the data suggests that this is the remit of heroic team leaders. For insight on this front, we must look to a different type of exemplary leader: finance's sage.

5 Sages Support Admiration through Organization

Sages are paragons of wisdom. Their store of knowledge appears limitless. Their wise counsel – often addressing issues of practical, moral relevance – is invaluable for many. This characterization is typical of sages in classic literatures (Novak, 1995; Kiriyama and Ouchi, 2000; Uusimaki, 2018). And it is no different in the dataset: Participants repeatedly express admiration for the value that sages bring to the financial workplace. A senior technology professional describes his team's advice as "wise, sage counsel" (P15); a wealth-management associate looks up to "those who are more experienced" than him (P12); a retail analyst says she relies on the "wisdom" of others (P21); and a human-resources associate notes that his role model, an "inspirational boss," has a "super smart way" of navigating challenges and "bring[ing] something really different" to the organization (P24).

Sages, of course, vary across times and cultures. This seems to be true of sages in UK finance, as well. I identify two subtypes in the data: Founder Sages, who are deeply admired by employees; and Big Bank Sages, who infuse moral purpose into organizations, often doing so behind the scenes and typically through a wise use of company rhetoric. Both subtypes embody an other-regarding form of wisdom, including a purposeful type of leadership that helps colleagues make moral sense of their work (Zu, 2019). Both subtypes tell us something about the admiration involved in leading by example. But Big Bank Sages suggest that another positive emotion – *elevation* felt toward moral ideals – may also be important.

In this section, I offer a portrait of the industry's sages. I propose that, among the exemplar-types described in this Element, the sage in particular underscores how organizational structures – mainly associated with language – contribute to the effectiveness of leading by example. I substantiate this claim through three subthemes, or propositions, that align with the data. First, sages transmit wisdom through speech that, in turn, helps team members become more other-regarding. As participants suggest, the specific kind of wisdom that sages advance gives teammates something greater than themselves to work toward (Section 5.1). Second, moral development is strengthened through personal encounters with sagacious leaders. When regularly exposed to Founder Sages in particular, participants report outsized effects in thought, speech, and emotional response (Section 5.2). Third, organizational values are indispensable for the making of *other* leadership exemplars. Within large financial institutions especially, Big Bank Sages recognize that proper engagement with organizational values does not create passive followers or carbon copies of existing exemplars. Instead, it encourages team members to become exemplary leaders in their own right (Section 5.3). I close the section by summarizing my subthemes and by considering the purpose-giving function of wise organizational leaders (Section 5.4).

5.1 Sages Speak Wisdom and Give Purpose

To appreciate sages' distinct features, especially their other-regarding orientation, I look first to their vicious counterpart, "the genius with a thousand helpers" (P25). As described by a sagacious executive of an investment firm, the genius sits "at the top" of an organization and presumes to "know best." "The thousand helpers," he continues, "are just there" to do what the genius wants. The genius thus creates

> a very disempowering environment. And as long as the genius knows what to do and [is] ... successful, then the whole thing works. But without the genius, the whole thing ... falls to pieces, which is why you find ... so many organizations not actually being able to transition from one generation to the next. (P25)

Indeed, sometimes knowing what something *is* (the sage) is best achieved by knowing what it *is not* (the "genius"). In the account above, I observe in the "genius" a lack of three strengths of character. First, humility. The presumption of knowing best counters humility's openness to new information (Tangney, 2000; Chancellor and Lyubomirsky, 2013). Second, courage. The risk assumed in the genius's ego-centric business model displays rashness, a deficiency of courage (Aristotle, 350 BC/2009, bk. III). Finally, practical wisdom. As Aquinas (1266/1964) might say, the genius lacks wisdom precisely because he fails "to apply right reason to [his] actions" (pt. II-II, q. 47, a. 4). In this context, right reason would consider not only individual success but also the good of others (Palanski and Yammarino, 2007; Grossmann, Dorfman, and Oakes, 2020). Whatever the sage-type might be, it is *not* an exemplar that lets arrogance, rashness, and self-interest gain the upper hand.

That said, the dataset is not silent about what sagacious leaders are like. Indeed, the executive above gives a strong indication that industry sages are fundamentally other-regarding. His description of the genius is given as a negative example of "servant leadership," an ideal that the executive aspires to uphold: "this idea of service – that I'm here ultimately not to be the boss and make all the decisions, [but] to serve my team – ... is incredibly important," he says (P25). This statement supports his earlier claim regarding the financial profession itself: to "use your talents to generate capital [is to] live a life of service for other people" (P25).

The notion of service appears often in participants' accounts of sagacious figures. These accounts may also be self-referential. A company founder says this of his own decision to enter alternative investments:

> There's an opportunity to make a lot of money. And what's really interesting about money is that you can do really interesting things with it. So, I ... thought: Could you ... create a crosspollination ... where a high-caliber team ... can use ... some of that raw talent to get involved in the third sector? (P10)

In this reflection, practical wisdom's other-regarding orientation is apparent in at least two ways. The most obvious pertains to the ideal of serving others through the third, or charitable, sector. A second way involves employee incentivization, an underlying intuition about how to bring out the best, both professionally and personally, from his team (Schwartz, 2011). Here, the characterological differences between the founder and the genius are clearly seen: The founder motivates through collaborative "crosspollination" (P10), while the genius "disempower[s]" through ego (P25).

So, the sage characteristically displays a prosocial or other-regarding form of practical wisdom. But, as the data suggest, there is not just one type of sage within finance. A distinction is suggested by the different sizes of organizations in which sages lead. The sages described above – those whom I call *Founder*

Sages – own and manage organizations with small headcounts. But participants across the dataset describe sagacious figures (or their own sagacious qualities) within much larger organizations, as well. *Big Bank Sages* are often, but not always, in middle or senior/executive positions. They are also seemingly ubiquitous, albeit behind the scenes. Consider these reflections from seasoned baking professionals.

> [To do my job well,] firstly, [I need] a sense of purpose. We are here to serve ... The role of a bank is not to make money for shareholders. It is to provide finance to help the economy and help people prosper. [This] is our purpose. (P27)

> I would like to look back on my career and think [that] I've made a difference ... I don't just want to have made a difference to divisional targets ... I'd like to [have made] a difference to the country. (P17)

> [Leadership, for me, means] showing people the purpose of what we're about. It's about setting a direction. It's about engaging and motivating people to ... carry out the things that we're here to carry out: ... to help ... and make a difference. (P14)

Each excerpt displays a concern for the good of others – advanced through the "economy," "country," or "people" (P27, P17, P14) – and so reflects wisdom's other-regarding orientation, especially as expressed in Aristotle's (350 BC/2009) claim that wisdom extends to social fields, including economics, politics, and law (bk. VI.8). This social emphasis aligns Big Bank Sages with their Founder Sage counterparts.

However, an important difference is discerned: When Big Bank Sages speak of wisdom, they characteristically use the language of "purpose" – the purpose of an individual (P27), of banks in general (P27), or of their bank in particular (P14, P4). In contrast, Founder Sages speak wisdom by recalling their *own* stories – "bootstrap stor[ies]," as one founder calls them (P25) – thereby detailing their social aspirations without repeatedly using the word "purpose" in their accounts. Big Bank Sages thus appear more reliant on rhetoric – that is, an "ability to identify the available means of persuasion" to convey a point (Holt, 2006, p. 1672) – than entrepreneurial founders.

One reason for this effort may involve regulatory pressures that seem to be felt more strongly by traditional banks than by the alternative-investments organizations of the dataset's Founder Sages. In the data, for instance, a senior manager states that his company's purpose and values were relaunched due to a "*diktat* from the regulator*"* (P7). None of the Founder Sages mention the same pressure.

The emphasis on purpose may also be due to practical wisdom itself. Big Bank Sages operate in highly complex organizations. A senior leader remarks that, at any point in time, her company may have tens of thousands of permanent and temporary staff to motivate and develop (P18). In this context, wisdom – with its aim of helping individuals deliberate well in particular circumstances (Aristotle, 350 BC/2009, bk. VI.5) – is vital. Through prudential trial and error, Big Bank Sages may have found that clear purpose statements are strongly "sense-giving" (Kempster, Jackson, and Conroy, 2011). In other words, they resonate more strongly with a global workforce than the idiosyncratic and culturally specific stories of individuals: "we're four out of five, . . . people's connection to [our purpose] is very high," states a chief officer (P22). The *lingua franca* of purpose may be a prized fruit of these sages' practical wisdom.

5.2 Proximity to Sages Generates Outsized Effects

Of course, the idiosyncratic stories of, or about, Founder Sages are by no means ineffective for moral development. One participant, an investment associate, recounts the following about his boss: "I've … seen [him] … forego an economic benefit in order to maintain integrity … It's usually the grey areas where you see these virtues come out" (P29). Despite its brevity, this story highlights the pedagogical function – and perhaps effectiveness – of exemplarist narratives. As Moberg and Seabright (2000) note, ethical stories expand the "moral imagination" and so enrich one's sensitivity to ethical issues (p. 846). In his story, the associate connects investments with virtue, doing so against the backdrop of moral ambiguity. This is an important moral lesson, one that the associate deems worthy to share. While I have no way to verify whether the boss's example is actually followed, it is plausible to think that the story itself has some resonance in the associate's moral imagination (otherwise, why did he mention it?). Whether or not it is acted upon, the story certainly has made a moral impression.

Apart from stories, Founder Sages have enormous influence through language in general. Indeed, the more vivid parts of their vocabularies are often imitated by their teams. Across one small business, sages spoke with a somewhat mythical air, pointing to the "inner life" of leaders (P16) and reminding others that "character is destiny" (P25). Such language carries with it thick normative concepts that Founder Sages bestow, whether intentionally or not, upon their organizations. Once adopted by employees, this "ordinary language" helps employees make sense of a range of values in the workplace (Van der Linden and Freeman, 2017, p. 355). For instance, the investment associate (from the paragraph above) navigates "integrity" and "economic benefit" through the ordinary language of virtue. At the end of his story, he even repeats his boss's characterological question: "What kind of person do you want to be known for?" (P29). No surprise, then, that his firm is where employees hear that "character is destiny" (P25).

Sheer physical presence is another way in which Founder Sages – who continue to work in their firms – influence moral development. One sage, for instance, is praised for holding frequent office hours and for sitting in an open space to make himself available. He's a "good listener," the investment associate says reflectively (P29). Delving deeper into the significance of physical proximity, a sage himself notes how flying around the world to meet clients – specifically to confess poor investment decisions to them – is extremely important. It exhibits "humility," he says. And humility, he later continues, "is a really, really important part of any working environment" (P10).

Implied in these remarks is a general point concerning the importance of modeling virtues through leadership. But, more specifically, the physical presence of sages – whether to clients or to colleagues – is significant to note since it may contribute to the effectiveness of sages' example. Consider Croce and Vaccarezza's (2017) claim that "close-by" exemplars are more likely to elicit admiration than "distant" saints who are further removed from ordinary experience (p. 13). Although the point is made metaphorically, speaking to relatability (more relatable exemplars are "close" to the learner), it may be taken in a literal sense as well. Indeed, personal encounters (direct, first-person experiences) with exemplars are a recognized means of effective moral learning. As Kidd (2019) notes, they have particular advantages, including "a greater degree of empirical complexity" from which to learn and "greater opportunities for dialogue" with the exemplar (p. 371). The analyst, who worked directly for the sage that flew around the world, might corroborate this claim: "[our founder] works really hard ... And I *see* that his values are bigger than him," she says. "That's why I find him ... [to be] my primary role model" (P33, emphasis added).

Given the overall proximity to their teams (through stories, language, and physical presence), Founder Sages appear to have an outsized effect upon moral development. Employees recognize fundamental changes in thought ("[there's] a reorientation of how you think" [P16]), speech ("the language I use is ... different" [P19]), and identity ("It was a bit of a[n] ... epiphany for me" [P29]). These changes, of course, may result from other factors (e.g., positive work environments) and not from direct engagement with sages themselves. But the frequency of personal encounters with Founder Sages cannot be overlooked ("[Our founder] is very open with his time" [P29]). Nor can one deny the frequent stories of participants directly benefitting from sages ("He offered me a [job]" [P33]; "[our founder] gave [me] the opportunity to join" [P1]).

In fact, as Engelen et al. (2018) note, stories that showcase the beneficiaries of an exemplar are more potent than those that focus on the exemplar alone: The former elicits an "enhanced emotional involvement" from hearers (p. 353). In the case of Founder Sages, participant accounts almost always feature beneficiaries, who are often the storytellers themselves. Perhaps this dual role, as storyteller *and* beneficiary, helps explain the strongly emotive character of the following participant's reflection:

> [Our founder] is probably one of the most, if not the most, impressive individuals I've met in my life. Probably for the values that he has, for the gentleman that he is, for the success that he's had, for his philanthropic endeavors, for his wisdom. For the love and praise and grace that he shows to anybody who crosses his path, whether that's professionally or personally. Just a remarkable man. (P3)

Thus far, one might get the impression that sages, or exemplars in general, only elicit positive emotions from followers. But certainly, this can't be the case. Hence, an important question must be raised: What about the *negative* emotions involved in role modeling – for instance, the shame felt by observers when they compare themselves to, or are compared with, an exemplar (Vaccarezza and Niccoli, 2019)? Do sages account for these seemingly inevitable feelings? On this front, my verdict is mixed.

In the dataset, several participants (often women) express shame or frustration when certain colleagues (often men) are held out as exemplary and they are not. For example, the alternative-investments analyst singles out colleagues who "quite rightly ... shout about" their individual outputs and, in turn, are rewarded with "bonuses and ... advancement" (P33). For her, their self-promotion is "quite right" because their work is exceptional. Nevertheless, she cannot help but moan – "Oh, god" –since she believes in the value of "team outputs" and so expects cooperative behavior and collective rewards: "[it's] one team, one fight; we all contribute in different ways" (P33).

Here, "negative exemplarity-related emotions" may operate (Vaccarezza and Niccoli, 2019, p. 332). And sages would do well to prevent the type of frustration expressed above by showcasing – in certain circumstances – only "distant" exemplars: those "who are too far from the [observer's] experience to elicit in them defective forms of negative emotions" (Vaccarezza and Niccoli, 2019, p. 341). In other words, sages – or anyone involved in performance management – should resist crude, public comparisons between current employees. As the analyst suggests, cultures that brazenly "say who's best in the team" (P33) may undermine role modeling's positive affections and imitative effects: Observers may become despondent and leave.

Notably, however, participants rarely express negative emotions when describing sages or lessons learned from them. This may suggest that a well-functioning culture – being tied to Founder Sages specifically – may operate in the background, even as observers struggle with other supposed or simply bad exemplars in the workplace. Ogunfowora's (2014) suggestion thus holds: We need "multi-level" conceptualizations of role modeling that determine the importance of a role model's "proximity" to observers *vis-à-vis* observers' moral development (p. 1486). The investment analyst states that her boss, a Founder Sage, is her "primary role model" (P33). But perhaps their firm's self-promoting "exemplars," who may be "closer" to her on a daily basis, have shaped her moral attitudes in unrecognized ways. Whatever the case, an exploration of exemplar-proximity would need to consider the multiple channels through which sagacious exemplars influence moral development in organizations. Although not physically present at every moment, Founder Sages may be "close-by" in entangled and culturally bound ways.

5.3 Rhetoric Plays a Role in Exemplar Development

For Big Bank Sages, overly critical and even gushing remarks about their influence are more or less absent in the dataset. However, this does not mean that Big Bank Sages are less morally influential than their Founder Sage counterparts. Sages at large firms *do* bring about moral change: They do so primarily through the rhetoric of purpose.

How this is done is suggested by a senior leader as she describes the method by which purpose was established in, and broadcasted throughout, her organization:

> We didn't start . . . by saying, "Let's define our purpose statement." We asked ourselves . . ., "If we didn't exist . . ., what difference would it make in the world?" . . . We then interviewed . . . hundreds of clients across our footprint markets . . . [as well as] loads of people inside the bank. (P18)

Afterwards, she explains, the senior leaders came together to look at the data. They chose one positive word to characterize the bank's purpose. "This [word] is what [we want] our clients to tell us when we are at our best," she says. But purpose, she continues, is not enough: It addresses the *why* of the bank (why the bank exists), but not the *how* (how the bank behaves when it achieves its end). Thus,

> we ran . . . a crowd-sourcing exercise, leveraging technology, . . . to come up with our [company values] . . . We design[ed our] value[s] . . . [And these] help us become a [good] bank, in service of our purpose. (P18)

Company values, then, form part of a sage's rhetoric of purpose. As the officer puts it, they are "in service of . . . purpose" (P18). However, one wonders whether purpose-and-values rhetoric shapes moral development in a significant way.

An investment associate is skeptical: "in theory [we live out the values]," she says, " . . . in practice, I don't think [they] come through" (P30). Looking elsewhere for moral guidance, she finds "amazing people" – "leaders" who are "patient," "trustworthy," and "care about their team" – and she "maximizes [her] exposure to them" (P30). Addressing the (in)effectiveness of values as well, a director at a different bank speaks frankly: "Well, I'm just going to say it. I have to be honest. I don't take . . . notice of [the company values] at all" (P13). If people want to be moral, she says, then they should just "respect each other for [their] differences, . . . backgrounds, and [their] unique perspectives" (P13). This position corroborates the reflection of a broker – a novice – from another firm: "I don't actually remember seeing any posters saying, 'These are [our] values' . . . I guess [they're] just [in] . . . people's characteristics" (P2). Is rhetoric, then, a costly waste? Have Big Bank Sages invested too much for meager returns?

In Section 3.1, I show that novices tend to ignore, or perhaps take for granted, company values. But participant data suggest that not everyone does. In large firms especially, there are interviewees who appear to learn from, or at least seriously consider, the normative concepts built into company rhetoric. Take, for instance, this senior stockbroker who, while expressing frustration with company values (they get in the way of revenue generation, he suggests), betrays a moral lesson learned:

> Personally, I think I buy into the spirit of the values. I understand why they're there and the purpose they're trying to serve. But . . . we need to be . . . clearer on how we make . . . trade-offs [between the values and financial reward]. (P32)

This account may be usefully contrasted with the investment associate who saw his boss "forego an economic benefit in order to maintain integrity" (P29). In the associate's situation, a Founder Sage exemplified virtue, illustrating in concrete detail how values could be put into action. In the stockbroker's situation, no sage was physically present. Instead, the broker was given a moral framework – company values, curated by Big Bank Sages – and he himself had to learn how to utilize that framework well.

Might the broker's situation – this learning opportunity – have been part of the intentional design of Big Bank Sages? It appears so. Later in her interview, the senior leader describes how her firm encourages managers to "grow and evolve" into ethical leaders: "we get leadership development done in bite-sized chunks." Leadership, she continues, "is a muscle that you need to develop . . .

everyday," not through a "five-day residential . . . at Harvard or Oxford" (P18). In other words, moral learning happens through "get[ting] . . . involved in the day to day" (P20), which, as MacIntyre (2007) might note, helps to systematically extend "human powers to achieve [moral] excellence" (p. 187).

There is an important pedagogical lesson here – one that potentially challenges the importance of role modeling, or leading by example, for moral development. Already, I suggested that company values can be thought of as "transpersonal moral ideals" (see Section 3.1). And I gestured toward Kristjánsson's (2017) position that ideals themselves can motivate people to develop morally: The emotion of *elevation* – the type of moral awe that arises from experiences of moral ideas, rather than encounters with moral persons – is in large part responsible for this (p. 32). Following Kristjánsson (2017), I now add that this Platonic form of moral development should include practical advice on how to cultivate elevation "in a reflective, *phronesis*-sensitive way" (p. 35). In other words, elevation should not be blindly followed: It must be critiqued in an appropriate manner and, eventually, truly owned.

To wrestle with moral frameworks as the stockbroker does (P32) or to exercise leadership daily as the senior officer prescribes (P18) – each method provides opportunities to "test and learn" (P4) and "change [one's] habits" (P23), that is, opportunities where motivating emotions can be reflected upon in a practically wise manner (Aristotle, 350 BC/2009). Importantly, neither of these methods requires the presence of an exemplar. Lacking a concrete person to imitate, employees who genuinely engage with "the spirit of the values" (P32) have a certain latitude to become leaders of their own making (in this latter regard, they echo the moral curation typical of novices: see Section 3.1). And if they do this well, they will likely elicit the admiration of others and thereby become exemplary leaders in their own right. Again, this appears to be the sage's intent. "Character . . . is implicit in a lot of the design work we have done [in leadership training]," the senior officer notes (P18). No longer is it only "the HR lady who talks about purpose." Now, it is most company employees – especially those who know that "they need to change and grow and evolve if they want to be leaders of the future" (P18). Fortunately for these colleagues, Big Bank Sages provide the organizational means for moral learning to happen.

5.4 Summary and Discussion: Sages as Purposeful Leaders

We now take stock. Through three subthemes, my account of the sage-type suggests that:

1. *Sages speak wisdom and give purpose.* Finance's sage is not a "genius with a thousand helpers," but a "servant leader" (P25). Fundamentally other-regarding

(Grossmann, 2017), sages serve their organizations by empowering colleagues to use their talents freely and for a purpose that is greater than any one individual. Sages themselves supply this purpose through their language: Founder Sages motivate through personal stories, Big Bank Sages inspire with company rhetoric. Both means are strongly "sense-giving" (Kempster, Jackson, and Conroy, 2011). Both means fulfill one of wisdom's basic tasks in finance: to connect people through purpose.

2. *Proximity to sages generates outsized effects*. Founder Sages still work in their firms, and they appear to have significant effects upon employee character. They influence through stories that expand the "moral imagination" (Moberg and Seabright, 2000, p. 846); through vocabulary that conveys rich normative concepts (Van der Linden and Freeman, 2017); and through physical presence that provides opportunities for colleagues to learn directly from them (Kidd, 2019). Participants report outsized effects in thought, speech, and identity. The stories of those who have directly benefitted from a Founder Sage, for example through job opportunities or extra support, may elicit an "enhanced emotional involvement" from hearers (Engelen et al., 2018, p. 353). But Founder Sages, and anyone involved in performance management, should avoid crude comparisons between colleagues. Otherwise, they risk unduly eliciting "negative exemplarity-related emotions" (Vaccarezza and Niccoli, 2019, p. 332).

3. *Rhetoric plays a role in exemplar development*. Big Bank Sages influence others through company rhetoric, including the dissemination and repetition of their firm's purpose- and values-statements. While novices are skeptical of values, participants who actively engage with the values (e.g., in business transactions) appear to learn from them. This suggests that some firms have effective means by which colleagues can wrestle with, and learn from, "transpersonal moral ideals" in "*phronesis*-sensitive" ways (Kristjánsson, 2017, pp. 32, 35).

When it comes to leading by example, novices highlight the importance of admiration and heroes stress the contribution of empathy. By contrast, the sage exemplar-type illustrates how leading by example can operate – and operate *well* – when accounted for through organizational structures. Sages lead through wisdom; and they embed that wisdom into their organizations in various ways. Perhaps the most prominent means involves the use of language, including "bootstrap" stories from Founder Sages (P25) and company rhetoric from their Big Bank counterparts. Both methods elicit positive, morally motivating emotions in followers. Whatever the means and emotions involved, the moral aim of industry sages is clear: They work to give colleagues a sense of "purpose" (P18), a reason for being in finance that both transcends "mak[ing] a lot of money" (P10) and allows financiers to "live a life of service for other people" (P25). We might say, then, that finance's sages are purposeful, or purpose-*giving*, leaders. Allow me to briefly comment upon this characterization to draw together and expand upon some of the exemplarist claims raised in this section.

First, consider the quality, or nature, of the purpose that sages give to their colleagues and organizations. As illustrated by the Founder Sage who distinguishes "servant leadership" from "the genius with a thousand helpers" (P25), sagacious purpose is fundamentally selfless and other-regarding. This feature closely aligns finance's sages with archetypal sages in classic literatures. Consider, for example, chapter 7 of the *Tao Te Ching* (c. 400 BC/1996), one of Taoism's foundational texts:

> Heaven lasts long, and Earth abides.
> What is the secret of their durability?
> > Is it not because they do not live for
> > themselves,
> that they can live so long?
> Therefore, the Sage wants to remain behind.
> > But finds himself at the head of others.
> Reckons himself out,
> > but finds himself safe and secure.
> Is it not because he is selfless
> > that his Self is realized?

Indeed, because of their selflessness, industry sages realize their "Self," securing their standing within their organizations. And, through the admiration directed toward them, they provide the emotional and motivating conditions for colleagues to imitate their selfless intent.

This sounds well and good. But what exactly is praiseworthy or admirable about the selfless purpose of industry sages? I think there are two features of sagacious purpose that draw colleagues' moral attention. The first pertains to *transcendence*: Sages give others a transcendent moral purpose, one that exists outside of oneself and outside of one's firm. As suggested by seasoned professionals, such purpose may involve advancing the good of the "economy," "country," or "people" (P27, P17, P14). It is neither merely other-regarding nor narrowly restricted to one's team, for example (cf., heroic empathy); instead, it is expansive and transcendent. Perhaps there is a certain moral awe, even sublimity, associated with its scope and ambition (Clewis, 2015). The second feature involves *immanence*: Sages offer colleagues an immanent moral purpose. By this, I mean a purpose that implicates the working conditions of colleagues, including their sense of meaning and autonomy, as experienced in the here and now. To enjoy an immanent moral purpose is to be empowered at work, to engage in exciting "crosspollination" (P10), and to appreciate the "difference ... [one makes] in the world" (P18).

Considered together, the notions of transcendence and immanence can enrich our understanding of the appeal of finance's purpose-*giving* leaders. The purpose they give meets basic spiritual needs: As Potts (2022) might say, when finance professionals "aim at good and worthy ends," they realize "personally meaningful experiences" and thus fulfill their "self-transcendent visions" (p. 16). My analysis suggests that those visions are supplied, in no small way, by sagacious leaders. The purpose sages give meets other human needs in the workplace, as well. For instance, Zu (2019) suggests that the recent adoption of purpose across industries is correlated with improvements in employee brain health and overall well-being. And, drawing upon diverse philosophical traditions, Kempster et al. (2011) argue that "fidelity to a worthy purpose" is vital for a "good human life" (p. 321). Indeed, sagacious purpose is deeply human. Being holistic, it favors neither an overly spiritualized notion of purpose nor a mundane interpretation that would focus upon "divisional targets" at the expense of meaningful service (P17). So, as my discussion suggests, finance's sages are admired in part due to the compelling nature of their offer – that is, the purpose they give which they themselves model through their leadership.

Let me now address an ambiguity in the discussion above. I claimed that purposeful leaders (i.e., *persons*) elicit the admiration of their followers: This statement implies that they themselves – or some aspect of their personal traits or behaviors – are the object of admiration. But I also suggested that moral purpose (i.e., an *ideal*), including its transcendent and immanent dimensions, appeals to followers: Moral purpose helps shape and even constitutes their moral vision. In these two claims, we encounter that perennial contention between exemplary persons and "transpersonal moral ideals" (Kristjánsson, 2017, p. 32). And again, we question whether we must choose between these paths of moral formation.

If we choose persons over ideals (as some novices might do), then we seem to lack concepts to explain and justify our admiration. If we choose ideals over persons (as some must do, given the hiddenness of certain sages), then we rob ourselves of examples of ideals lived in real life (compare Sections 3.1 and 5.3). Of course, it must be admitted that this choice is artificial. Both exemplary persons and moral ideals are appropriate means of moral learning. It must also be acknowledged that both means are implicated in exemplarist moral learning, that is, the sort of learning involved in leading by example. After all, the stories of Founder Sages do not merely elicit admiration for the *persons* admired; the stories elicit positive emotions related to the *ideas* – including purposes – that the founders represent.

A more significant point follows from this realization. Considering my study's emotive lens, I now ask whether sages might have a "doubly" positive effect upon followers' moral development: Founder Sages, in particular, awe with tales of daring and wisdom, thereby eliciting the emotion of *elevation* in their colleagues; they also model what daring and wisdom could look like in actual fact, thus eliciting *admiration* from would-be sages. As the emotional correlates of ideals and exemplars (Haidt, 2003; Kristjánsson, 2017), could elevation and admiration operate in tandem in the same act of leadership by example? If so, the characterological effects may be tremendous. In a sector characterized by vice and negativity, a double helping of positivity and sagacious virtue would be welcome.

6 Conclusion

This Element offered a descriptive and normative analysis of leadership exemplars in UK finance. It challenged the common trope that finance is morally bankrupt. But, more significantly, it offered an empirically informed account of what it means to lead ethically and by example.

The Element's dataset consisted of thirty-three interviews conducted in 2021 with financial services professionals, representing various job roles and industry subsectors in the UK. And its research method featured Braun and Clarke's (2021) reflexive approach to thematic analysis, a Big Q qualitative method that values the subjectivity and interpretive expertise of the researcher. The Element asked two sets of questions: (i) Who did participants admire and in what leadership contexts, and (ii) how did admiration respond vis-à-vis the leaders identified? To answer these questions and, more generally, to make sense of the data, the Element developed a theoretical lens, LBE, based on Linda Zagzebski's philosophy of moral exemplarism. Offered as a comprehensive ethical theory, moral exemplarism defines "all central terms in moral discourse including 'virtue,' 'right act,' 'duty,' and 'good life,' by direct reference to exemplars, or persons *like that*, where *that* is the object of admiration" (Zagzebski, 2017, p. 3, emphasis in original). Leadership by Example can thus be conceptualized as an application of Zagzebski's theory: It identifies the objects of participants' admiration (leadership exemplars), and it suggests that moral discourse – about positive leadership in finance – should be understood in relation to participants' exemplars.

So, who did participants admire? My analysis featured three themes that I conceptualized as three types of leadership exemplar. The first leadership exemplar is the novice. Underappreciated in various literatures, novices excel in self-leadership (Neck and Manz, 2013); and they stand out for their curiosity with respect to personal, moral development. Novices also underscore the fact that leading by example relies upon the emotion of admiration: no admiration of exemplars, no leading by example. In support of this proposition, and to expand upon it, the novice-type speaks to three exemplarist claims. First, the curious prefer learning from exemplars. If novices had to choose between abstract methods of moral development (e.g., engaging with company values) and personal encounters with positive leaders, novices would characteristically choose the latter (Section 3.1). Second, humility is a complementary and even prerequisite virtue for curiosity. Novices succeed in sourcing morally relevant information because they are humble (Section 3.2). Third, curiosity needs moral guidance. A strong sense of integrity – aided by moral questioning – helps novices discern good from bad examples (Section 3.3). Novices themselves elicit the admiration of colleagues in the workplace. As one participant suggests, emerging leaders in finance should be novice-like in character: "I would want them to be curious. I would want them to ask questions" (P13).

The second exemplar-type is the hero. Heroes in finance are courageous, but they are most admired for their prosocial form of empathy as witnessed in team contexts. With regard to leading by example, heroes suggest that leadership role modeling is strengthened by the empathic abilities of exemplars themselves: Empathic leaders *feel* the admiration directed toward them and, in response, they continue to *act* virtuously. This exemplar-type speaks to three exemplarist claims: that finance is emotionally "fraught" (P6), and so heroes must deal with and not ignore their colleagues' emotions (Section 4.1); that heroes display a prosocial form of empathy, one that supports teammates in difficult times (Section 4.2); and that empathy is rewarded with admiration that begets more empathy: This phenomenon may be referred to as the empathy–admiration loop, and it may be a fundamental aspect of leading by example as it highlights an important social incentive for ethical behavior (Section 4.3).

The final leadership exemplar is the sage. Sages give colleagues a transcendent moral purpose (a purpose that transcends the self and even the firm) as well as an immanent moral purpose (a sense of autonomy and responsibility in one's role). Sages thus embody an other-regarding form of wisdom. Whether Founder Sages (leaders of small firms) or Big Bank Sages (who operate behind the scenes in large organizations), the sage-type in general underscores how language-based organizational structures contribute to the effectiveness of leading by example. This point is substantiated through three exemplarist claims. First, sages transmit wisdom through speech – including "bootstrap" stories (P25) – which helps colleagues become other-regarding (Section 5.1). Second, moral development is strengthened through personal encounters with sagacious leaders. Participants report outsized effects in thought, speech, and emotional response when exposed to Founder Sages (Section 5.2). Third, organizational values play an important role in forming leadership exemplars. Within large organizations especially, Big Bank Sages recognize that thoughtful engagement with organizational values does not create carbon copies of existing exemplars. It instead encourages employees to become exemplary in their own right (Section 5.3).

An important question to ask about my analysis is whether its claims are propositional (i.e., normative) or merely descriptive. After all, if my analysis presented what interviewees said was the case, then shouldn't we admit that its leadership insights are mere descriptions and *not* propositions to follow? I appreciate the skepticism but insist that my analytical insights go beyond mere description. They do so because of my theoretical lens (LBE) and its underlying normative theory, moral exemplarism. Allow me to explain.

Following Zagzebski (2017), we might say that this Element's analysis is like a map, something that gives us an "understanding of the domain of morality" (p. 7) through a presentation of three exemplar-types. The types indicate what the moral terrain of UK finance looks like, but the types themselves are morally insufficient. Other parts of the map may exist (e.g., additional exemplar-types not addressed in my analysis). And other maps of the same location may be available (e.g., deontological principles concerning what should, or should not, happen in leadership in finance). That said, the current map – that is, my thematic analysis – is morally suggestive. We can understand its suggestiveness in at least two ways.

The first way pertains to moral discourse and the motives of participants' exemplars. Having interpreted participant accounts through a "hermeneutics of empathy" (Braun and Clarke, 2021, p. 160), my analysis draws out what participants themselves consider to be admirable. With this information in hand, we can begin to identify what it is about exemplars x, y, and z that make them objects of admiration and thus worthy of imitation. So, what exactly should we admire in the novice, hero, and sage? According to Zagzebski (2017), we should admire their *motives* or, more technically put, their "motive disposition[s]" – that is, their "disposition[s] to have a distinctive emotion that initiates and directs action toward a [characteristic] *end*" (p. 108, emphasis added). My analysis illuminates important motive dispositions for each exemplar-type: Novices, through curiosity, tend toward the end of personal development and thereby excel in self-leadership; heroes, through empathy, tend toward the end of supportive care for colleagues and thus exemplify positive team leadership; sages, through wisdom, tend toward the end of purpose-giving and hence are exemplary leaders of purposeful financial organizations. What we admire, then, are exemplars' teleologically directed motives – and not necessarily their specific actions that may be immoral if unsuccessfully replicated in certain situations.

Moreover, we can *classify* their motives according to virtue (curiosity, empathy, and wisdom) and can understand those virtues in specific leadership contexts (self, team, and organizational leadership). Such categorization equips our moral discourse and reasoning with useful normative concepts, and this helps improve the successful transferability of exemplary motives into our own circumstances. So, for instance, I admire novices for their curiosity and, wanting to follow their example, apply that type of curiosity to my own moral development. However, I do *not* attempt to apply it to an organizational act of purpose-giving (the sage's remit) since doing so might risk confusing followers with my seemingly muddled quest in ethical experimentation.

Thus, my analysis is normatively suggestive in the sense that Zagzebski's theory prescribes: It identifies admirable motives, including intelligible moral ends, and it invites us to consider how those motives may be transferred into our own situations. Such consideration will likely involve normative concepts that are implicated in, or baked into, an exemplar's motive disposition. And so, the act of deriving an "ought" from an exemplar's "is" is not an illogical move: Engaging with an exemplar means engaging with the moral concepts, ends, and arguments that the exemplar is seen to represent and/or implicate.

With regard to the specifics of my analysis, it is up to the reader to determine whether the arguments made and concepts implicated are morally sound: It is not within the scope of this Element to make a definitive case. That said, my analysis begins moral reflection, and discerning readers may have plenty of questions to raise. Some questions may be about the psychological dynamics of leading by example: For instance, one may ask whether it is admiration or curiosity that motivates novices to morally develop (Section 3.1). Other questions may concern the underlying normative implications of particular observations: Does the empathy–admiration loop betray a nascent egoism on the part of self-aware exemplars (Section 4.3)? Do Founder Sages threaten employees with moral authoritarianism (Section 5.2)? Are Big Bank Sages as morally libertarian as my analysis suggests (Section 5.3)? These are important questions that future research, including empirically informed philosophical analyses, should tackle.

A second way in which my analysis is morally suggestive also follows from Zagzebski's theory. It can be succinctly stated. In short, by focusing upon the emotion of admiration, my analysis – in theory – is morally motivating: After all, "admiration motivates emulation of admired persons" (Zagzebski, 2017, p. 8).

To this claim, one might say that my analysis is not actually motivating; that it merely identifies and describes admiration in a specific place and time; and that it is an observation, not a moral exhortation. But these are reductive characterizations of both my analysis and its theoretical lens. The analysis itself offers three exemplarist narratives (one per exemplar-type); and "narratives are ... the basic way humans ... develop and alter their moral sensibilities ... [as they] capture the imagination and elicit emotions that motivate action" (Zagzebski, 2017, p. 8). My narratives may not be as engaging as Pulitzer Prize journalism, but I hope that their depth and breadth engaged readers intellectually and on an emotional level.

Further to this, by applying my theoretical lens (LBE) to this dataset, we get a sense of what leading by example might look like not only from exemplar-specific perspectives (from the vantage points of novices, heroes, and sages) but also from bigger perspectives that are unexplored in this Element. For instance, we might imagine what leading by example looks like on an intra-organizational plane, wherein various exemplar-types learn from and challenge each other to reach new professional and personal heights. We might also imagine LBE not as a mere lens, but as a mature philosophical or social scientific construct, through which we would say that LBE *must* entail curiosity, humility, and integrity (Section 3); courage and empathy (Section 4); an other-regarding form of wisdom (Section 5); and so on to be considered truly or consistently ethical. These are grand and inspiring "narratives" of a certain kind. They activate our moral imagination and elicit within us emotions that aim toward action – for instance, an intellectual awe that moves us to engage further in empirical and conceptual research.

And, indeed, further research is required. This Element offered but one interpretation of a rich dataset of interviews on character and leadership in UK finance. Other interpretations can be offered using the *exact same* qualitative method – reflexive thematic analysis – deployed in this Element. This possibility is one of the strengths of Braun and Clarke's approach: No analysis will be the same, as each depends on the hermeneutic sympathies, theoretical commitments, and subjectivity of the researcher. I think that my analysis has something worthwhile to say about leading by example. But, to conclude, it is worth reiterating that my analysis has something even more significant to say for the field of leadership studies in general – namely, that empirical data can be interrogated in insightful and disciplinarily appropriate ways when qualitative research is embraced for its philosophical potential and underlying ethical orientation. In other words, we can greatly advance our understanding of leadership if we examine the evidence not from the isolated perspective of a technician, but from the empathic lens of the humanities.

References

Algoe, S. B. and Haidt, J. (2009). Witnessing Excellence in Action: The "Other-praising" Emotions of Elevation, Gratitude, and Admiration. *Journal of Positive Psychology*, 4(2), 105–127. https://doi-org.ezproxy-prd.bodleian.ox.ac.uk/10.1080/17439760802650519.

Aquinas, T. (1266/1964). *Summa Theologiae*. Edited by English Dominicans, London: Blackfriars.

Aristotle. (350 BC/2009). *Nicomachean Ethics*, new ed. Edited by L. Brown, translated by W. D. Ross, Oxford: Oxford University Press.

Augustine. (400/1992). *Confessions*. Translated by H. Chadwick, Oxford: Oxford University Press.

Bandura, A. (1977). *Social Learning Theory*, Englewood Cliffs, NJ: Prentice-Hall.

Bass, B. M. and Riggio, R. E. (2006). *Transformational Leadership*. 2nd ed, Mahwah, NJ: L. Erlbaum Associates.

Bett, R. (1989). The Sophists and Relativism. *Phronesis*, 34(1–3), 139–169. https://doi.org/10.1163/156852889X00107.

Boje, D. M. (1991). The Storytelling Organization: A Study of Story Performance in an Office-Supply Firm. *Administrative Science Quarterly*, 36(1), 106–126. https://doi.org/10.2307/2393432.

Braun, V. and Clarke, V. (2006). Using Thematic Analysis in Psychology. *Qualitative Research in Psychology*, 3(2), 77–101. https://doi.org/10.1191/1478088706qp063oa.

Braun, V. and Clarke, V. (2019). Reflecting on Reflexive Thematic Analysis. *Qualitative Research in Sport, Exercise and Health*, 11(4), 89–597. https://doi-org.ezproxy-prd.bodleian.ox.ac.uk/10.1080/2159676X.2019.1628806.

Braun, V. and Clarke, V. (2021). *Thematic Analysis: A Practical Guide*, Los Angeles, CA: SAGE.

Braun, V., Terry, G., Gavey, N., and Fenaughty, J. (2009). "Risk" and Sexual Coercion among Gay and Bisexual Men in Aotearoa/New Zealand: Key Informant Accounts. *Culture, Health & Sexuality*, 11(2), 111–124. https://doi.org/10.1080/13691050802398208.

Brenton, H. (2024). Britain's Next Financial Crash Is Coming. This Time It Won't Be the Banks. *Politico*. www.politico.eu/article/britains-next-financial-crash-is-coming-this-time-it-wont-be-the-banks/. (Accessed: March 18, 2025).

Brown, M. E., Treviño, L. K., and Harrison, D. A. (2005). Ethical Leadership: A Social Learning Perspective for Construct Development and Testing. *Organizational Behavior and Human Decision Processes*, 97(2), 117–134. https://doi.org/10.1016/j.obhdp.2005.03.002.

Businessolver (2022). *State of Workplace Empathy*. West Des Moines, IA: Businessolver. www.businessolver.com/workplace-empathy/. (Accessed: February 19, 2024).

Byrne, D. (2022). A Worked Example of Braun and Clarke's Approach to Reflexive Thematic Analysis. *Quality & Quantity*, 56(3), 1391–1412. https://doi.org/10.1007/s11135-021-01182-y.

Chancellor, J. and Lyubomirsky, S. (2013). Humble Beginnings: Current Trends, State Perspectives, and Hallmarks of Humility. *Social and Personality Psychology Compass*, 7(11), 819–833. https://doi-org.ezproxy-prd.bodleian.ox.ac.uk/10.1111/spc3.12069.

Ciulla, J. B. (2019). The Two Cultures: The Place of Humanities Research in Leadership Studies. *Leadership*, 15(4), 433–444. https://doi.org/10.1177/1742715019832145.

Clarke, V. and Braun, V. (2019). How Can a Heterosexual Man Remove His Body Hair and Retain His Masculinity? Mapping Stories of Male Body Hair Depilation. *Qualitative Research in Psychology*, 16(1), 96–114. https://doi.org/10.1080/14780887.2018.1536388.

Clewis, R. R. (2015). *The Kantian Sublime and the Revelation of Freedom*, Cambridge: Cambridge University Press.

Croce, M. and Vaccarezza, M. S. (2017). Educating through Exemplars: Alternative Paths to Virtue. *Theory and Research in Education*, 15(1), 5–19. https://doi-org.ezproxy-prd.bodleian.ox.ac.uk/10.1177/1477878517695903.

Darwall, S. (1998). Empathy, Sympathy, Care. *Philosophical Studies*, 89(2/3), 261–282. https://doi.org/10.1023/a:1004289113917.

Davis, D. E., Worthington, E. L., and Hook, J. N. (2010). Humility: Review of Measurement Strategies and Conceptualization as Personality Judgment. *The Journal of Positive Psychology*, 5(4), 243–252. https://doi-org.ezproxy-prd.bodleian.ox.ac.uk/10.1080/17439761003791672.

Duan, C. and Hill, C. E. (1996). The Current State of Empathy Research. *Journal of Counseling Psychology*, 43(3), 261–274. https://doi.org/10.1037/0022-0167.43.3.261.

Duan, C. and Sager, K. (2016). Understanding Empathy: Current State and Future Research Challenges. In C. R. Snyder, Lopez, S. J., Edwards, L. M., and Marques, S.C. eds., *The Oxford Handbook of Positive Psychology*, 3rd ed., Oxford: Oxford University Press, pp. 533–550.

Engelen, Bart, Alan Price Thomas, Alfred Archer, and Niels van de Ven. 2018. "Exemplars and Nudges: Combining Two Strategies for Moral Education." *Journal of Moral Education* 47 (3): 346–365. https://doi.org/10.1080/03057240.2017.1396966.

Frohman, A. L. and Johnson, L. W. (1993). *The Middle Management Challenge: Moving from Crisis to Empowerment*, New York: McGraw-Hill.

Gentry, W. A. Cullen, K. L., Sosik, J. J., Chun, J. U., Leupold, C. R., and Tonidandel, S. (2013). Integrity's Place among the Character Strengths of Middle-level Managers and Top-level Executives. *The Leadership Quarterly*, 24(3), 395–404. https://doi.org/10.1016/j.leaqua.2012.11.009.

George, B. (2008). Failed Leadership Caused the Financial Crisis. *U.S. News and World Report*, 19 November. www.usnews.com/opinion/articles/2008/11/19/failed-leadership-caused-the-financial-crisis. (Accessed: March 18, 2025).

Gibson, D. E. (2004). Role Models in Career Development: New Directions for Theory and Research. *Journal of Vocational Behavior*, 65(1), 134–156. https://doi.org/10.1016/S0001-8791(03)00051-4.

Gjerde, S. and Alvesson, M. (2020). Sandwiched: Exploring Role and Identity of Middle Managers in the Genuine Middle. *Human Relations*, 73(1), 124–151. https://doi.org/10.1177/0018726718823243.

Goetz, J. and LeCompte, M. (1984). *Ethnography and Qualitative Design in Educational Research*, Orlando, FL: Academic Press.

Greenleaf, R. K. and Spears, L. C. (2002). *Servant Leadership: A Journey into the Nature of Legitimate Power and Greatness*, 25th anniversary ed., New York: Paulist Press.

Grossmann, I. (2017). Wisdom in Context. *Perspectives on Psychological Science*, 12(2), 233–257. https://doi.org/10.1177/1745691616672066.

Grossmann, I., Dorfman, A., and Oakes, H. (2020). Wisdom Is a Social-ecological Rather Than Person-centric Phenomenon. *Current Opinion in Psychology*, 32, 66–71. https://doi.org/10.1016/j.copsyc.2019.07.010.

Haidt, J. (2003). Elevation and the Positive Psychology of Morality. In J. Haidt and C. I. Keyes, eds., *Flourishing: Positive Psychology and the Life Well-lived*. Washington, DC: American Psychological Association, pp. 275–289.

Henderson, E. (2022). The Educational Salience of Emulation as a Moral Virtue. *Journal of Moral Education*, 53(1), 73–88. https://doi.org/10.1080/03057240.2022.2130882.

Hildebrand, C. (2023). Feeling, Cognition, and the Eighteenth-century Context of Kantian Sympathy. *British Journal for the History of Philosophy*, 31(5), 974–1004. https://doi.org/10.1080/09608788.2023.2174949.

Hoch, J. E. Bommer, W. H., Dulebohn, J. H., and Wu, D. (2018). Do Ethical, Authentic, and Servant Leadership Explain Variance above and beyond Transformational Leadership? A Meta-Analysis. *Journal of Management*, 44(2), 501–529. https://doi.org/10.1177/0149206316665461.

Hoffman, M. L. (1984). The Contribution of Empathy to Justice and Moral Judgment. In N. Eisenberg, ed., *The Development of Prosocial Behavior*. New York: Academic Press (Developmental Psychology Series), pp. 281–313.

Holt, R. (2006). Principals and Practice: Rhetoric and the Moral Character of Managers. *Human Relations*, 59(12), 1659–1680. https://doi.org/10.1177/0018726706072867.

House, R. (1977). A 1976 Theory of Charismatic Leadership. In J. G. Hunt and L. L. Larson, eds., *Leadership: The Cutting Edge*. Carbondale, IL: Southern Illinois University Press, pp. 189–207.

Hurley, J. (2023). Latest Delay Alarms Victims of HBOS Reading Scandal. *The Times*, 24 July. www.thetimes.co.uk/article/latest-delay-alarms-victims-of-hbos-reading-scandal-bhsmttmx9. (Accessed: March 18, 2025).

Hurtado, P. (2023). Ex-Goldman Banker Ng Seeks Celebrity Prison for 1MDB Fraud. *Bloomberg*, 21 March. www.bloomberg.com/news/articles/2023-03-21/ex-goldman-banker-ng-seeks-celebrity-prison-for-1mdb-fraud. (Accessed: March 18, 2025).

İnan, İ. (2012). *The Philosophy of Curiosity*, London: Routledge.

Jefferson, T. (1771/1975). Letter to Robert Skipwith. In M. D. Peterson, ed., *The Portable Thomas Jefferson*. New York: Penguin Books, pp. 349–351.

Kay, J. (2015). *Other People's Money: Masters of the Universe or Servants of the People?* London: Profile Books.

Kempster, S., Jackson, B., and Conroy, M. (2011). Leadership as Purpose: Exploring the Role of Purpose in Leadership Practice. *Leadership*, 7(3), 317–334. https://doi.org/10.1177/1742715011407384.

Kidd, I. J. (2019). Admiration, Attraction and the Aesthetics of Exemplarity. *Journal of Moral Education*, 48(3), 369–380. https://doi-org.ezproxy-prd.bodleian.ox.ac.uk/10.1080/03057240.2019.1573724.

Kiriyama, S. and Ouchi, R. (2000). *21st Century: The Age of Sophia: The Wisdom of Greek Philosophy and the Wisdom of the Buddha*, Tokyo: Hirakawa Shuppan.

Klein, K. and Hodges, S. D. (2001). Gender Differences, Motivation, and Empathic Accuracy: When It Pays to Understand. *Personality & Social Psychology Bulletin*, 27(6), 720–730. https://doi.org/10.1177/0146167201276007.

Kripke, S. (1980). *Naming and Necessity*, Cambridge, MA: Harvard University Press.

Kristjánsson, K. (2017). Emotions Targeting Moral Exemplarity: Making Sense of the Logical Geography of Admiration, Emulation and Elevation. *Theory and Research in Education*, 15(1), 20–37. https://doi.org/10.1177/1477878517695679.

Lanchester, J. (2015). *Capital*, London: Faber & Faber.

Le, H. Schmidt, F. L., Harter, J. K., and Lauver, K. J. (2010). The Problem of Empirical Redundancy of Constructs in Organizational Research: An Empirical Investigation. *Organizational Behavior and Human Decision Processes*, 112(2), 112–125. https://doi.org/10.1016/j.obhdp.2010.02.003.

Lee, S. and Kim, H. (2021). An Empirical Study on Verbal Violence Experiences among Bank Consulting. *Turkish Journal of Computer and Mathematics Education*, 12(10), 970–977. https://turcomat.org/index.php/turkbilmat/article/view/4278. (Accessed: January 23, 2024).

Lewis, M. (2015). *Flash Boys: Cracking the Money Code*, London: Penguin Books.

Luo, G. (2004). *Three Kingdoms: A Historical Novel*. Translated by M. Roberts, Berkeley: University of California Press.

Luthans, F. and Avolio, B. (2003). Authentic Leadership: A Positive Developmental Approach. In K. S. Cameron, J. E. Dutton, and R. E. Quinn, eds., *Positive Organizational Scholarship: Foundations of a New Discipline*. San Francisco, CA: Berrett-Koehler, pp. 241–261.

Luyendijk, J. (2013). At the Back of Your Mind Is: I Have to Hit My Target, or There's Redundancy. *The Guardian*. www.theguardian.com/commentisfree/joris-luyendijk-banking-blog/2013/sep/19/target-redundancy-banking-fixed-income. (Accessed: March 18, 2025).

Luyendijk, J. (2015). *Swimming with Sharks: My Journey into the World of Bankers*, London: Guardian Books.

Macaskill, A., Maltby, J., and Day, L. (2002). Forgiveness of Self and Others and Emotional Empathy. *The Journal of Social Psychology*, 142(5), 663–665. https://doi.org/10.1080/00224540209603925.

MacIntyre, A. (2007). *After Virtue: A Study in Moral Theory*, 3rd ed., Notre Dame, IN: University of Notre Dame Press.

Maibom, H. (2022). *The Space between: How Empathy Really Works*, New York: Oxford University Press.

Maile, A. (2024). Open-mindedness and Phenomenological Psychopathology: An Intellectual Virtue Account of Phenomenology and Three Educational Recommendations. *Philosophical Psychology*, 38(1), 304–330. https://doi.org/10.1080/09515089.2024.2379987.

Malterud, K. (2016). Theory and Interpretation in Qualitative Studies from General Practice: Why and How? *Scandinavian Journal of Public Health*, 44(2), 120–129. https://doi.org/10.1177/1403494815621181.

Matava, R. (2011). "Is," "Ought" and Moral Realism: The Roles of Nature and Experience in Practical Understanding. *Studies in Christian Ethics*, 24(3), 311–328. https://doi-org.ezproxy-prd.bodleian.ox.ac.uk/10.1177/0953946811405912.

McKinsey & Company (2023). *How Empathy Has Transformed and Empowered Ademola's Journey.* www.mckinsey.com/careers/meet-our-people/careers-blog/ademola. (Accessed: March 18, 2025).

Mhatre, K. and Riggio, R. (2014). Charismatic and Transformational Leadership: Past, Present, and Future. In D. V. Day, ed., *The Oxford Handbook of Leadership and Organizations*. Oxford: Oxford University Press, pp. 221–240.

Miles, M., Huberman, A., and Saldaña, J. (2020). *Qualitative Data Analysis: A Methods Sourcebook*, 4th ed., Los Angeles, CA: SAGE.

Mill, J. (1984). High and Low Self-monitoring Individuals: Their Decoding Skills and Empathic Expression. *Journal of Personality*, 52(4), 372–388. https://doi.org/10.1111/j.1467-6494.1984.tb00358.x.

Miscevic, N. (2007). Virtue-based Epistemology and the Centrality of Truth (Towards a Strong Virtue-Epistemology). *Acta Analytica: Philosophy and Psychology*, 22(3), 239–266. https://doi.org/10.1007/s12136-007-0011-z.

Moberg, D. J. (2000). Role Models and Moral Exemplars: How do Employees Acquire Virtues by Observing Others? *Business Ethics Quarterly*, 10(3), 675–696. https://doi.org/10.2307/3857898.

Moberg, D. J. (2008). Mentoring for Protégé Character Development. *Mentoring & Tutoring*, 16(1), 91–103. https://doi.org/10.1080/13611260701801056.

Moberg, D. J. and Seabright, M. (2000). The Development of Moral Imagination. *Business Ethics Quarterly*, 10(4), 845–884. https://doi.org/10.2307/3857836.

Neck, C. P. and Houghton, J. (2006). Two Decades of Self-leadership Theory and Research: Past Developments, Present Trends and Future Possibilities. *Journal of Managerial Psychology*, 21(4), 270–295. https://doi.org/10.1108/02683940610663097.

Neck, C. P. and Manz, C. C. (2013). *Mastering Self-leadership: Empowering Yourself for Personal Excellence*, 6th ed., Boston, MA: Pearson.

Novak, P. (1995). *The World's Wisdom: Sacred Texts of the World's Religions*, New York: HarperSanFrancisco.

Nowell, L. S. Norris, J. M., White, D. E., and Moules, N. J. (2017). Thematic Analysis: Striving to Meet the Trustworthiness Criteria. *International Journal of Qualitative Methods*, 16(1), 1–13. https://doi.org/10.1177/1609406917733847.

Ogunfowora, B. (2014). It's All a Matter of Consensus: Leader Role Modeling Strength as a Moderator of the Links between Ethical Leadership and Employee Outcomes. *Human Relations*, 67(12), 1467–1490. https://doi.org/10.1177/0018726714521646.

Osterman, P. (2008). *The Truth about Middle Managers: Who They Are, How They Work, Why They Matter*, London: McGraw-Hill.

Palanski, M. and Yammarino, F. (2007). Integrity and Leadership: Clearing the Conceptual Confusion. *European Management Journal*, 25(3), 171–184. https://doi.org/10.1016/j.emj.2007.04.006.

Park, R., Vyver, J., and Bretherton, R. (2020). The Humble Leader: Understanding Perceptions and Implications of Humility in Leadership. *European Journal of Applied Positive Psychology*, 4, 1–12. www.nationalwellbeingservice.org/volumes/volume-4-2020/volume-4-article-14/. (Accessed: March 18, 2025).

Peterson, C. and Seligman, M. (2004). *Character Strengths and Virtues: A Handbook and Classification*, Washington, DC: American Psychological Association.

Pickens, C. and Braun, V. (2018). "Stroppy Bitches Who Just Need to Learn How to Settle"? Young Single Women and Norms of Femininity and Heterosexuality. *Sex Roles*, 79(7–8), 431–448. https://doi.org/10.1007/s11199-017-0881-5.

Pixley, J. (2004). *Emotions in Finance: Distrust and Uncertainty in Global Markets*, Cambridge: Cambridge University Press.

Potts, G. (2022). *Work as a Calling: From Meaningful Work to Good Work*, London: Routledge.

Preston, S. D. (2007). A Perception-Action Model for Empathy. In T. Farrow and P. Woodruff, eds., *Empathy in Mental Illness*. Cambridge: Cambridge University Press, pp. 428–447.

Preston, S. D. (2016). Neural and Physiological Mechanisms of Altruism and Empathy. In C. R. Snyder et al., Lopez, S. J., Edwards, L. M., and Marques, S. C., *The Oxford Handbook of Positive Psychology*, 3rd ed., Oxford: Oxford University Press, pp. 754–772.

Preston, S. D. and de Waal, F. (2002). Empathy: Its Ultimate and Proximate Bases. *Behavioral and Brain Sciences*, 25(1), 1–72. https://doi.org/10.1017/S0140525X02000018.

Putnam, H. (1975). The Meaning of "Meaning". In H. Putnam, ed., *Philosophical Papers: Mind, Language and Reality*. Cambridge: Cambridge University Press, pp. 215–271.

Reynders, P., Kumar, M., and Found, P. (2022). "Lean on Me": An Integrative Literature Review on the Middle Management Role in Lean. *Total Quality*

Management & Business Excellence, 33(3–4), 318–354. https://doi.org/10.1080/14783363.2020.1842729.

Robinson, B. (2016). Character, Caricature, and Gossip. *The Monist*, 99(2), 198–211. https://doi.org/10.1093/monist/onv036.

Roca, E. (2008). Introducing Practical Wisdom in Business Schools. *Journal of Business Ethics*, 82(3), 607–620. https://doi.org/10.1007/s10551-007-9580-4.

Rocchi, M., Ferrero, I., and Beadle, R. (2021). Can Finance Be a Virtuous Practice? A MacIntyrean Account. *Business Ethics Quarterly*, 31(1), 75–105. https://doi.org/10.1017/beq.2020.5.

Sanchez, P. (2018). The Secret to Leading Organizational Change Is Empathy. *Harvard Business Review*, 20 December. https://hbr.org/2018/12/the-secret-to-leading-organizational-change-is-empathy. (Accessed: March 18, 2025).

Sartre, J. (1946/1973). *Existentialism and Humanism*. Translated by P. Mairet, London: Eyre Methuen.

Schwartz, B. (2011). Practical Wisdom and Organizations. *Research in Organizational Behavior*, 31, 3–23. https://doi.org/10.1016/j.riob.2011.09.001.

Sison, A., Ferrero, I., and Guitián, G. (2017). Characterizing Virtues in Finance. *Journal of Business Ethics*, 155(4), 995–1007. https://doi-org.ezproxy-prd.bodleian.ox.ac.uk/10.1007/s10551-017-3596-1.

Skapinker, M. (2023). "From SVB to the BBC: Why Did No One See the Crisis Coming?" *Financial Times*, 19 March. www.ft.com/content/4d589d5c-f2cb-4568-93dd-acda6fab931f. (Accessed: March 18, 2025).

Smith, A. (1776/2008). *An Inquiry into the Nature and Causes of the Wealth of Nations: A Selected Edition*. Edited by K. Sutherland, Oxford: Oxford University Press.

Sriram, N. and Greenwald, A. G. (2009). The Brief Implicit Association Test. *Experimental Psychology*, 56(4), 283–294. https://doi.org/10.1027/1618-3169.56.4.283.

Stempel, J. (2023). Sam Bankman-Fried Will Not Face a Second Trial. *Reuters*, 30 December. www.reuters.com/legal/sam-bankman-fried-will-not-face-second-trial-us-prosecutors-say-2023-12-29/. (Accessed: March 18, 2025).

de Swaan, J. C. (2020). *Seeking Virtue in Finance: Contributing to Society in a Conflicted Industry*, Cambridge: Cambridge University Press.

Szutta, N. (2019). Exemplarist Moral Theory – Some Pros and Cons. *Journal of Moral Education*, 48(3), 280–290. https://doi-org.ezproxy-prd.bodleian.ox.ac.uk/10.1080/03057240.2019.1589435.

Tangney, J. P. (2000). Humility: Theoretical Perspectives, Empirical Findings and Directions for Future Research. *Journal of Social and Clinical Psychology*, 19(1), 70–82. https://doi.org/10.1521/jscp.2000.19.1.70.

The Big Short (2015). [Blu-ray]. Directed by Adam McKay. United States: Paramount Pictures.

Toussaint, L. and Webb, J. (2005). Gender Differences in the Relationship between Empathy and Forgiveness. *The Journal of Social Psychology*, 145(6), 673–685. https://doi.org/10.3200/SOCP.145.6.673-686.

Tzu, L. (c. 400 BC/1996). *Tao-Teh-Ching: A Parallel Translation Collection*. Edited by B. Bolsen, Boston, MA: Gnomad.

Uusimaki, E. (2018). The Rise of the Sage in Greek and Jewish Antiquity. *Journal for the Study of Judaism in the Persian, Hellenistic, and Roman Period*, 49(1), 1–29. https://doi.org/10.1163/15700631-12491185.

Vaccarezza, M. S. and Niccoli, A. (2019). The Dark Side of the Exceptional: On Moral Exemplars, Character Education, and Negative Emotions. *Journal of Moral Education*, 48(3), 332–345. https://doi.org/10.1080/03057240.2018.1534089.

Van der Linden, B. and Freeman, R. E. (2017). Profit and Other Values: Thick Evaluation in Decision Making. *Business Ethics Quarterly*, 27(3), 353–379. https://doi.org/10.1017/beq.2017.1.

Virgil. (2007). *Aeneid*. Translated by F. Ahl and E. Fantham, Oxford: Oxford University Press.

Watson, L. (2019). Educating for Inquisitiveness: A Case against Exemplarism for Intellectual Character Education. *Journal of Moral Education*, 48(3), 303–315. https://doi.org/10.1080/03057240.2019.1589436.

Watson, L. (2022). Cultivating Curiosity in the Information Age. *Royal Institute of Philosophy Supplement*, 92, 129–148. https://doi.org/10.1017/S1358246122000212.

Werpehowski, W. (2007). Practical Wisdom and the Integrity of Christian Life. *Journal of the Society of Christian Ethics*, 27(2), 55–72. https://doi.org/10.5840/jsce20072724.

Whitcomb, D. Battaly, H., Baehr, J., and Howard-Snyder, D. (2017). Intellectual Humility: Owning Our Limitations. *Philosophy and Phenomenological Research*, 94(3), 509–539. https://doi.org/10.1111/phpr.12228.

Zagzebski, L. (2003). Emotion and Moral Judgment. *Philosophy and Phenomenological Research*, 66(1), 104–124. https://doi-org.ezproxy-prd.bodleian.ox.ac.uk/10.1111/j.1933-1592.2003.tb00245.x.

Zagzebski, L. (2004). *Divine Motivation Theory*, Cambridge: Cambridge University Press.

Zagzebski, L. (2006). The Admirable Life and the Desirable Life. In T. Chappell, ed., *Values and Virtues: Aristotelianism in Contemporary Ethics*, Oxford: Clarendon, pp. 53–66.

Zagzebski, L. (2013). Moral Exemplars in Theory and Practice. *Theory and Research in Education*, 11(2), 193–206. https://doi-org.ezproxy-prd.bodleian.ox.ac.uk/10.1177/1477878513485177.

Zagzebski, L. (2017). *Exemplarist Moral Theory*, New York: Oxford University Press.

Zu, L. (2019). Purpose-driven Leadership for Sustainable Business: From the Perspective of Taoism. *International Journal of Corporate Social Responsibility*, 4(1), 1–31. https://doi.org/10.1186/s40991-019-0041-z.

Acknowledgments

This Element was made possible through the support and efforts of friends and colleagues from the Virtues and Vocations research group and from the Faculty of Theology and Religion at the University of Oxford. My deepest gratitude to each and every one of you. I look forward to celebrating your future successes. I am especially grateful to The Lord Biggar CBE, principal investigator of the original Virtues and Vocations grant, and to the McDonald Agape Foundation and Christ Church, Oxford, for supporting my academic work. Finally, to the interviewees who took time out of their busy schedules: thank you. I hope this Element shines light on your exemplars and inspires you to become even more exemplary in your personal and professional lives.

This publication was made possible through the support of a grant from the John Templeton Foundation, Grant Number: 61413. The opinions expressed in this publication are those of the author and do not necessarily reflect the views of the John Templeton Foundation.

Cambridge Elements

Leadership

Ronald E. Riggio
Claremont McKenna College

Ronald E. Riggio, Ph.D. is the Henry R. Kravis Professor of Leadership and Organisational Psychology and former Director of the Kravis Leadership Institute at Claremont McKenna College. Dr. Riggio is a psychologist and leadership scholar with over a dozen authored or edited books and more than 150 articles/book chapters. He has worked as a consultant and serves on multiple editorial boards.

Susan E. Murphy
University of Edinburgh

Susan E. Murphy is Chair in Leadership Development at the University of Edinburgh Business School. She has published numerous articles and book chapters on leadership, leadership development, and mentoring. Susan was formerly Director of the School of Strategic Leadership Studies at James Madison University and Professor of Leadership Studies. Prior to that, she served as faculty and associate director of the Henry R. Kravis Leadership Institute at Claremont McKenna College. She also serves on the editorial board of The Leadership Quarterly.

Georgia Sorenson
University of Cambridge

The late Georgia Sorenson, Ph.D., was the James MacGregor Burns Leadership Scholar at the Moller Institute and Moller By-Fellow of Churchill College at Cambridge University. Before coming to Cambridge, she founded the James MacGregor Burns Academy of Leadership at the University of Maryland, where she was Distinguished Research Professor. An architect of the leadership studies field, Dr. Sorenson has authored numerous books and refereed journal articles.

Advisory Board

Neal M. Ashkanasy, *University of Queensland*
Roya Ayman, *Illinois Institute of Technology*
Kristin Bezio, *University of Richmond*
Richard Boyatzis, *Case Western Reserve University*
Cynthia Cherrey, *International Leadership Association*
Joanne Ciulla, *Rutgers Business School*
Barbara Crosby, *University of Minnesota*
Suzanna Fitzpatrick, *University of Maryland Medical Center*
Al Goethals, *University of Richmond*
Nathan Harter, *Christopher Newport University*
Ali Jones, *Coventry University*
Ronit Kark, *Bar-Ilan University*
Kevin Lowe, *University of Sydney*
Robin Martin, *University of Manchester*
Stella Nkomo, *University of Pretoria*
Rajnandini Pillai, *California State University, San Marcos*

Micha Popper, *University of Haifa*
Terry Price, *University of Richmond*
Krish Raval, *University of Oxford*
Roni Reiter-Palmon, *University of Nebraska*
Birgit Schyns, *Durham University*
Gillian Secrett, *University of Cambridge*
Nicholas Warner, *Claremont McKenna College*

About the Series

Cambridge Elements in Leadership is multi- and inter-disciplinary, and will have broad appeal for leadership courses in Schools of Business, Education, Engineering, Public Policy, and in the Social Sciences and Humanities.

In addition to the scholarly audience, Elements appeals to professionals involved in leadership development and training.

The series is published in partnership with the International Leadership Association (ILA) and the Møller Institute, Churchill College in the University of Cambridge.

Cambridge Elements

Leadership

Elements in the Series

Leading the Future of Technology: The Vital Role of Accessible Technologies
Rebecca LaForgia

Cultural Dynamics and Leadership: An Interpretive Approach
Nathan W. Harter

There Is More than One Way to Lead: The Charismatic, Ideological, and Pragmatic (CIP) Theory of Leadership
Samuel T. Hunter and Jeffrey B. Lovelace

Leading for Innovation: Leadership Actions to Enhance Follower Creativity
Michael D Mumford, Tanner R. Newbold and Samantha England

The Hazards of Great Leadership: Detrimental Consequences of Leader Exceptionalism
James K. Beggan, Scott T. Allison and George R. Goethals

The Gift of Transformative Leaders
Nathan O. Hatch

Ethical Leadership in Conflict and Crisis: Evidence from Leaders on How to Make More Peaceful, Sustainable, and Profitable Communities
Jason Miklian and John E. Katsos

Questioning Leadership
Michael Harvey

Peace Leadership: A Story of Peace Dwelling
Stan Amaladas

Network Leadership: Promoting a Healthier World through the Power of Networks
Jeffrey Beeson

Shared Leadership 2.0: Taking Stock and Looking Forward
Christina L. Wassenaar, Craig L. Pearce and Natalia Lorinkova

Leadership by Example
Edward A. David

A full series listing is available at: www.cambridge.org/CELE

For EU product safety concerns, contact us at Calle de José Abascal, 56–1°,
28003 Madrid, Spain or eugpsr@cambridge.org.

www.ingramcontent.com/pod-product-compliance
Lightning Source LLC
LaVergne TN
LVHW011856060526
838200LV00054B/4359